Jordan

GETTING THINGS DONE

JAMES MENDELSOHN

Twenty-First Century Books
Brookfield, Connecticut

Cover photograph courtesy of Frank Wolfe/LBJ
Library Collection

Photographs courtesy of LBJ Library Collection: pp. 2
(Frank Wolfe), 122 (Yoichi R. Okamoto), 140 (Frank
Wolfe); AP/Wide World Photos: pp. 11, 101, 147;
Hulton Getty/Liaison Agency: p. 24; © Corbis: pp.
27, 59, 94 (Jack Moebes), 102 (Flip Schulke), 161
(Owen Franken), 170 (Wally McNamee); The UT
Institute of Texan Cultures at San Antonio (No. EN
1956.1.11): p. 30; Barbara Jordan Archives, Texas
Southern University: pp. 35, 41, 51, 53, 71, 77, 167;
Phillis Wheatley Senior High School, Houston,
Texas: p. 62; Library of Congress: p. 67; UPI/Corbis-
Bettmann: pp. 87, 109, 163; Texas State Library and
Archives Commission: p. 134

Published by Twenty-First Century Books
A Division of The Millbrook Press, Inc.
2 Old New Milford Road
Brookfield, Connecticut 06804
www.millbrookpress.com

Cataloging-in-Publication Data is on file at the Library of Congress

Contents

For Erika, Elizabeth, Daniel, Maggie,
Rose, Nathan, and Sam

Something Is Different Tonight

By the summer of 1976, the United States had gone through seven years of political turmoil. The secret bombing of Cambodia, the Vietnam War, and most notably Watergate had made people distrust the government, especially the president. President Richard Nixon, a Republican, had resigned in disgrace just two years earlier, in 1974. The Democrats saw Nixon's fall from power as an opportunity to win back the presidency for the first time in eight years.

It was July 12, and the Democratic National Convention was under way in Madison Square Garden, New York City. Barbara Jordan stood on the speaker's platform before the largest crowd of people she had ever seen. She was about to give the second of two keynote addresses to the convention. The air around her was buzzing with the sounds of everyone speaking while red, white, and blue banners hung from the ceiling and from the sides of every wall. Everywhere she looked on the convention floor, there were delegates from the different states in the country, a great sea of people that covered every space, every aisle, and every seat. Jordan couldn't feel any breeze on her face, only a wave of heat that rose from the floor of the convention center, where people were milling about discussing politics. No wonder she felt nervous.

As keynote speaker, Jordan's task was to inspire these people to support the Democratic candidate for president, whoever they would nominate. Her job was to make Democrats as active and as dedicated as possible. That was not going to be easy. Moments before, Senator John Glenn had given the first keynote address, but the crowd had barely noticed him. Glenn, the first astronaut to have circled the earth in a spaceship, was still regarded as a national hero. In 1976 he was a rising star in the Democratic party. But the Democrats were hardly unified at the time, and the crowd had continued to talk among themselves in spite of Glenn's efforts to rally them. The noise of their talking drowned out Glenn's voice over the microphone and speakers. Now Jordan, a second-term congresswoman from Texas, had to do what Glenn couldn't, in a speech that was being televised to 75 million viewers nationwide.

Four years before, in 1972, Barbara Jordan had gained national attention. She was the first African American woman ever to be elected to Congress by a southern state. Then, in 1974, she electrified the nation when, as a member of the House Judiciary Committee, she gave a speech defining the grounds for impeachment of President Nixon. Whether for or against Nixon, all members of the House Judiciary Committee had given speeches. But Jordan's speech captured the essence of the controversy. In fifteen minutes, Jordan carefully, clearly, and masterfully laid out the ways in

Barbara Jordan acknowledges applause at the Democratic National Convention, July 13, 1976.

which Nixon's actions had violated the Constitution and identified the charges on which he should be tried. Before that moment, Texas newspapers had identified her only as a member of the liberal voting bloc in Congress, unusual among the mostly conservative representatives from Texas; after the speech, they described her as a powerful speaker and a passionate upholder of the Constitution.[1] That was why Robert Strauss, chairman of the Democratic National Committee and organizer of the Democratic convention, had asked her to give the keynote address.

Jordan had an extraordinary voice. She spoke in deep, resonant tones, enunciating precisely, and she could raise and lower her pitch expertly to tell a story or to emphasize a point. Still more impressive, her booming voice allowed her to project her words with remarkable intensity, as if her words were shot out of a cannon. Her voice brought people instantly to attention.

So did her size. Tall and broad, she was a commanding figure, which was fine with her. Although she was by nature a private person, she didn't want to be ignored; she wanted to be politically influential. In the months before her keynote address, she had lost nearly sixty pounds because the Houston newspapers had begun to describe her as a "hulking" figure rather than a powerful, imposing "presence."[2] (The newspapers did not make such comments about congress*men*.) For those who knew her, there was little doubt she was an impressive person.

If she was briefly nervous, it was nothing she couldn't handle. Her speech before the Judiciary Committee had been no fluke. She was a talented, experienced orator and a shrewd judge of her audience. She had been a champion debater in high school and college. Growing up, she had learned how to captivate an audience by watching her father preach in church. She believed she could make this crowd listen. She took a last step toward the speaker's podium and began to speak.

"One hundred and forty-five years ago," she declared, "the Democratic party met for the first time in convention to select their presidential candidate." She expected to get some delegates' attention, but to her surprise, the noisy arena went quickly silent, and the eyes of all the delegates turned toward the platform. Jordan was determined to take advantage of their sudden focus upon her. She spoke briefly about the longstanding tradition of the Democratic party convention. Then she paused to make the audience pay special attention to her next words.

"But there is something different about tonight," Jordan said. "There is something special about tonight. What is different? What is special?," she asked the crowd. Then she answered her own question. "I, Barbara Jordan, am a keynote speaker."

One hundred and forty-five years before, Barbara Jordan would never have been able to speak at such a convention because she was a woman and because she was black. Now she stood before the Democratic National Convention as one of the first African Americans elected to Congress in more than one hundred years. "My presence here," she declared, "is one additional bit of evidence that the American dream need not forever be deferred."

Jordan wasn't about to leave things at that. Her speech was not a celebration of her personal success. Now that the audience was truly listening, she began to bring everyone together, toward goals that were important for the success of the Democratic party. She told the delegates she wasn't going to speak about the problems of America at this time, and she wasn't going to waste time complaining about the Republicans. Instead she reminded them of what Democrats stood for: equality for everyone in the country. No one should be more privileged than another person. Democrats were dedicated to making the promise of America become a reality, she said. Jordan then listed the various ways in which the Democratic party had fought for equality for all, from voting rights legislation to fair-housing laws. These laws symbolized for Jordan what the American dream truly meant—not a chicken in every pot nor a car for every home. The American dream wasn't about guaranteeing material things for everyone. It was about equal opportunity for all.

Barbara Jordan paused a moment, giving her audience the chance to think about her words, and then she finished. "Now, I began this speech by commenting to you on the uniqueness of a Barbara Jordan making the keynote address. I am going to close my speech by quoting a Republican president and ask you to relate the words of Abraham Lincoln, relate them to the concept of a national community in which every last one of us participates: 'As I would not be a slave,'" she quoted Lincoln, "'so I would not be a master.'"

Slavery may have been outlawed 113 years before, but Jordan felt there were still "masters" to contend with. Too many people did not have an equal voice in shaping the direction of the country. Too many were trapped in poverty, unable to gain a political voice. She insisted that the United States be considered as one giant community in which every citizen might have full and equal voice. That was her idea of democracy.

"Whatever differs from this," she said, "to the extent of the difference, is no democracy."[3]

As the speech ended, so did the silence of the delegates. It was as if a storm of noise had suddenly appeared in the convention hall, thundering forth from the floor of the arena. The delegates clapped, stamped their feet, and shouted their approval until the sound was deafening. They chanted, "We want Barbara."

Jordan smiled and accepted the approval of the audience. She had done her job. Although the applause continued, she stepped down from the platform as Robert Strauss, the chairman of the Democrat National Committee, stepped up. He was smiling and asking the audience to quiet down. But nothing he said and no gesture he made could stop the delegates' applause. Finally, he gave up and called for Jordan to return to the platform. He cheered himself while Jordan laughed with delight.[4]

Soon Jordan retired to a back room in Madison Square Garden, from which she watched the convention on television. Jimmy Carter, the frontrunner for the Democratic nomination for president, called to ask for her support. Something historic had clearly happened. A black woman had declared her arrival in the arena of national politics, and she had acted as a leader, bringing together the forces of Democrats behind her vision of democracy.

In the next few days, all of the newspapers across the country declared that Barbara Jordan was the hit of the convention. *The Philadelphia Evening Bulletin* reported: "The Democrats were losing to boredom, 1–0, last night when they had the good sense to bring Barbara Jordan off the bench. Miss Jordan, as the ballplayers say, took it downtown. . . . Grand slam."

The New York Times wrote: "It is a classic American success story." Barbara Jordan's hometown newspaper, *The Houston Post*, declared: "A poor kid from Houston's Fifth Ward sealed her destiny as a national superstar. . . ."[5]

When Jimmy Carter was nominated by the Democrats to be their presidential candidate, many of the delegates said Barbara Jordan should be the vice-presidential candidate. It did not happen. But on the last night of the convention, as she stood beside Jimmy Carter and his vice-presidential candidate, Walter Mondale, the delegates still screamed, "We want Barbara."

Jordan spent the rest of the summer and the early fall campaigning for Carter and Mondale, who won the election that November. Then she returned to Congress. As Jimmy Carter prepared to take office, many thought Jordan would give up her position in Congress and become Director of the FBI or the U.S. representative to the United Nations. But Barbara Jordan decided she would leave Congress only if Carter offered her the position of head of the Department of Justice, the Attorney General of the United States. It did not happen.[6]

Within a year, Jordan made a surprising decision. She announced that she was going to retire from Congress when her term was over. In June of 1977, she was awarded an honorary degree and gave the commencement speech at the graduation ceremony for Harvard University. Before the students at Harvard, she urged all citizens to take charge of their government once more. Everyone should be able to influence the direction of the country, she declared; everyone should have a voice. Then, as suddenly as she had arrived on the national scene, she returned to Austin, Texas, to become a professor of public policy at the University of Texas.

*F*or a brief time, Barbara Jordan had seized the attention and stirred the feelings of the country. She had convinced almost everyone that the country could become better if everyone tried to make it so. She had come closer than any black woman ever to national office. Then she had suddenly and mysteriously resigned. During her six years in Congress, she had brought many citizens together to fight for equality for all. Now her work would continue, but more quietly—outside of Washington, away from the limelight of politics, where every ordinary citizen acted.

For the remainder of Barbara Jordan's life, people asked why she had cut short her political career. She refused to answer them. It was a matter of privacy, and Barbara Jordan believed in her privacy as much as she believed in the importance of political participation. She died without answering that question and without admitting publicly that her body had been ravaged first by multiple sclerosis, which placed her in a wheelchair for the last eight years of her life; and then by leukemia, which killed her. She surrounded herself with a group of loyal friends, their friendship based in part on their ability to keep her private life private.

Any story of Barbara Jordan's life must therefore focus largely on her public life, with which she wanted to be identified. From the time she arrived upon the political stage until her death in 1996, Barbara Jordan left us with virtual instructions for how she wished to be remembered. She wanted to be understood as a political figure and as a symbol for civil rights, for democratic participation, and for justice. She wanted to be remembered as a passionate defender of the Constitution. In the very language of her oratory, in the fierce pride her name evokes among many Americans—Texans in particular—she came to symbolize those ideals.

But people are not only symbols, and so there is a second kind of story to be told about her public life. While she pursued the most worthy of goals, Barbara Jordan was clearly human. She had a strong sense of duty to her ideals; but she was also practical-minded. She wanted to get something done in politics, and to get something done, she believed, she had to make compromises. Among those who shared her ideals, some critics believed that she compromised too much. They preferred that she be less practical and more idealistic. She had no tolerance for such remarks. She found ways to work with those who were her political opposites, conservatives in an age where conservatism often meant supporting segregation between blacks and whites. And therein lies the most compelling part of her story, her ability to get along with, if not befriend, people one might regard as her political enemies. Her public life shows that, like all powerful politicians, she moved between her need to compromise for practical purposes and her commitment to the ideals that made her act in such a practical fashion.

How did she feel about these compromises? What led her to become not only a figure of great inspiration but a political player in the backrooms of the U.S. Congress on Capitol Hill and the Texas Senate in Austin? What made her become this kind of person? Here our story moves further into the realm of speculation. We have only the bits and pieces she let be known about

All that development was far in the future when, in 1528, a small group of Spanish explorers, part of the Narvaez expedition, landed on the shores of Galveston Island in Galveston Bay and traveled inland to Buffalo Bayou.[2] Among them, historians report, was the first black to land in the territory, a Moroccan slave to the Spanish captain Andres Dorantes. We know him only by his first name, Estevanico.[3] The small group of explorers depended on each other for protection from both the weather and hostile Native Americans; so Estevanico became less a slave and more a partner in the expedition. In later years, as the Spanish empire conquered the Americas, Estevanico became an important translator between the Spanish and Native Americans, as well as a guide to the territory near the Rio Grande.

Over the next three hundred years, people of African heritage appear repeatedly among the inhabitants of a territory that was successively Indian, Spanish, Mexican, independent, and finally a part of the United States. A black bugler was part of the second Spanish military expedition to East Texas in 1691. Black soldiers manned the Spanish forts in the territory throughout the eighteenth century. A black weaver was among the free settlers of Bucareli, on the Trinity River, in 1776, the year the United States declared its independence. For more than 260 years, as Texas was settled, people of African ancestry were a significant part of the population. By 1792, Spanish Texas recorded 34 "Negroes" and 414 "mulattoes"—people they identified as having both Spanish and "Negro" heritage—out of 2,992 people. That meant nearly one sixth the population of Spanish Texas had African heritage.[4]

Born in Texas, Mexico, Spain, or Africa, these earliest black settlers lived in relative peace with Europeans and Native Americans long before the territory became part of the United States. Africans in Spanish Texas grew vegetables, built homes, married and raised their families. Both the Indians and the Spanish allowed Africans greater freedom than in colonial America or the newly formed United States. In fact, in 1823, when the newly formed Republic of Mexico took control of Texas territory, slavery was outlawed.[5] After 1803, many African Americans escaped plantation slavery in the southern United States for Spanish Texas, or they bought their freedom and then resettled either in Spanish Texas or among the Cherokee and Creek tribes who controlled the surrounding territory. Most of them, however, had to live in segregated communities among the Spaniards, and in general, they were not treated as equals among Native Americans. But they mixed and married with some of the Spanish, the Creek, and the Cherokee. Blacks in Spanish Texas or Native American territory were second-class citizens, but citizens nonetheless.

Those circumstances changed quickly when Texas became a republic in 1836, independent of both the United States and Mexico. During the preceding decades, southerners and pioneers from the United States had settled in Texas while it was still part of Mexico; many of them brought their slaves along. They then fought and won independence from Mexico. Although they valued their own independence and their own freedom, most people in the new Republic of Texas had far different ideas about the place of Africans in their society than the Spanish or the Mexicans. They were mostly slave owners who believed strongly that African Americans should be slaves, and that free blacks among them should be severely restricted because they might encourage runaways or start a rebellion among the slaves.[6]

Once they formed the Republic of Texas, these white settlers made sure African Texans could not vote or own property or mix with whites. They also forbade African Texans from testifying against whites in court cases, which made it impossible to use the courts to protect blacks against violence from white Americans. Without property or the right to vote, unprotected from violence at the hands of whites, people of African heritage in Texas saw the freedoms they had previously enjoyed vanish.

Few of these conditions changed when Texas became part of the United States in 1845. The United States Congress tried to banish free blacks from Texas.[7] Free blacks were forbidden to own guns, and they suffered criminal punishments whites did not, including branding and whipping.

During the Civil War, most white Texans fought for the Confederacy. Those whites who opposed the Confederacy were often silenced or driven from the state. Then, on June 19, 1865, two months after the war ended, Union troops marched into Texas and declared all slaves to be free. In spite of "Juneteenth," as that date came to be known, full citizenship for African Americans was never guaranteed. White Texans strongly resisted increasing freedom for African Americans. Under Texas laws, black people were still not allowed to testify against whites. Fearing the increased power and freedom of African Americans, whites organized themselves into marauding groups that regularly attacked and killed African Americans, as they did in

*Cotton pickers and overseer in Texas
in a print from around 1800*

many other southern states. Yet Texas law continued to forbid blacks to accuse white killers in a criminal trial. From 1865 to 1868, 468 free blacks were killed in Texas, many of them by vigilante groups such as the Ku Klux Klan.[8]

The U.S. government responded by sending in federal troops to protect African Americans and to restore law and order, an action that began the period known as "Reconstruction" in the South. With the help of the federally funded Freedman's Bureau, many black schools were established throughout the state. For the first time, African American males became state and federal legislators, policemen, and city councilmen. In Houston, the city council had several black members after 1869. But such progress was all but halted and soon reversed. In 1871 the Freedman's Bureau shut down in Texas, and federal troops began to leave. By 1877, Reconstruction had ended, and whites were again in control of the Texas state government.

In 1877—less than a lifetime from when Barbara Jordan was born—Texas and the rest of the South responded quickly to the absence of federal troops. They further segregated blacks and whites and denied African Americans the right to vote. So-called white-men's parties throughout Texas harassed, beat, and even murdered those blacks who attempted to vote or to be politically active. In the last quarter of the nineteenth century, African Americans gradually lost political representation in the Texas state and city governments. By 1899, blacks were shut out of the state legislature. Since slavery, little appeared to have changed. African Americans owned almost no farmland; they could not get a good education; and they had few decent jobs. As Texas industrialized, African Americans were shut out of all but the lowest-paying jobs.

The results of these circumstances were grim: In 1900, 63 percent of all employed black Texans worked in agriculture, as field hands and sharecroppers on white-owned farms. Fewer blacks in Texas earned wages from nonfarming jobs than in any other state in the Union.[9] After 1908, few African Americans participated in state and national elections.[10] For nearly three hundred years, black Texans had mingled, married, and helped to build the territory of Texas into a settlement of Spain, Mexico, and finally the United States. Freed blacks had expected to reap the rewards of their work and share in the growth of Texas. But the new political order thwarted any such hopes.

Barbara Jordan's hometown of Houston had become a vital part of growth in Texas. After it incorporated as a town in 1836, Houston was a business center for the cotton, rail, timber, and shipping industries for more than sixty years. A large proportion of its manual labor force consisted of African American slaves and, after the Civil War, free African Americans. Then, in the twentieth century, the city became a modern center for oil and petrochemicals, its population rising from 44,000 in 1900 to 400,000 in 1940. In that same time period, the African American population grew from 14,608 to more than 86,000 persons.[11]

But the vast majority of blacks in Houston, who had played such a vital role in building the city, did not share its newfound wealth. A chief reason they did not enjoy this greater prosperity was segregation, which had been a way of life in Houston since the 1870s. In 1896, in a landmark decision known as *Plessy* v. *Ferguson*, the Supreme Court of the United States ruled that segregation of the races was legal. According to that ruling, a state could have separate public facilities for black and white citizens and still be faithful to the Constitution of the United States, so long as those facilities were of equal worth. "Separate but equal" was the term by which we remember that decision—separate

Farmworkers picking cotton near Dallas, Texas, in 1907. Working conditions had hardly changed since cotton was first planted in the state.

schools, separate toilets, and separate drinking fountains. In the decades after Reconstruction, segregation had been the rule that was widely followed throughout the South and selectively followed in the North as well. *Plessy* v. *Ferguson* made segregation the law of the land until 1954.

By the time Barbara Jordan was born, segregation severely restricted African Americans in Houston, Texas. Schools in Houston were segregated in 1876, railroad cars in 1891, and streetcars in 1903; city hotels, restaurants, theaters, and public facilities followed in 1907, and parks in 1922—fourteen years before Barbara Jordan was born. In 1922, blacks and whites were forbidden to live in the same home. Cut off from the rest of the population, assigned to inferior schools, African Americans in Houston survived mostly on service jobs for the white population or for their own community. Women worked as maids, laundresses, cooks, and midwives.[12] Labor unions were highly segregated, so they offered only modest possibilities for blacks to advance. As late as 1940, 89.6 percent of black workers in Houston held jobs in the lowest categories of pay and prestige—as domestic servants, service workers, or unskilled and semiskilled laborers.[13]

Out of necessity, black communities developed in the areas neighboring downtown Houston, the Third Ward to the south and east, the Fourth Ward to the west, and the Fifth Ward to the northeast. These were the very areas in which Barbara Jordan and her family lived and that she eventually represented in the state senate and the U.S. Congress. For most African Americans in Houston in the early twentieth century, to live in these communities was to live in relative poverty. In

1940, when Barbara Jordan was four years old, 23.3 percent of black households did not have running water—four times the level of nonblack households. Many streets were unpaved and drained poorly, so that heavy rains left them flooded and impassable. Still, along San Felipe Street in the Fourth Ward a black business district developed, and a modest-sized, black middle class grew up, composed mostly of schoolteachers, a few professionals, and leaders of churches, the mainstay of the black community in the early twentieth century. Virtually all African Americans belonged to a church in those times. The black community developed its own clubs, libraries, hospitals, and other institutions, including the *Houston Informer* newspaper in 1919 and the Houston Negro Chamber of Commerce, which was founded in the mid-1930s. Nonetheless, with the exception of black-owned grocery stores, barber shops, and restaurants—businesses that catered exclusively to the black community—most jobs and money depended upon the white businesses of Houston.[14]

What might it have felt like to be an African American in early twentieth-century Houston? From all reports, African Americans felt as if they were living a life apart from the rest of the city. They also felt constantly humiliated by whites. By custom, an African American entered a white business or home only through the back door. African Americans often shopped in separate sections of white stores and waited for white customers to be served before they were. Black men and women were not allowed to try on clothing in white stores because whites considered them dirty. If a movie theater allowed African Americans, they were required to enter through a side door and to sit in the balcony. Blacks were expected to treat

*The "Negro Waiting Room" at the Katy Depot,
in San Antonio, Texas*

whites not only with respect but with deference, as if they were speaking with their superiors—even if they were speaking to a white person who was much younger than themselves. Whites commonly referred to African Americans by their first names, as if their proper names didn't matter—"boy," "uncle," or "Sal" were typical. And if a black person objected, he or she would be insulted and sometimes beaten.[15]

The police, who were virtually an all-white force, freely harassed African Americans on the street. They believed their duty was to keep African Americans in their place, apart from whites. Sometimes the police resorted to open brutality toward African Americans; at nearly all times they treated blacks with suspicion.

Such conditions sometimes led to violence. On August 23, 1917, African American soldiers of the Twenty-Fourth Infantry, stationed at nearby Camp Logan, responded forcefully to abuse they suffered at the hands of the Houston police. Most of the soldiers were from the North; they weren't used to such humiliation. On several occasions while visiting the San Felipe district of Houston, they had been harassed by the Houston police. Early on August 23, the Houston police broke up a craps game and allegedly beat and arrested a "Negro" soldier and a woman. They also beat and arrested a member of the "Negro" military police who insisted that the soldier be turned over to him for punishment. Rumor spread that the military policeman was dead. That evening, 125 to 150 black soldiers armed themselves and descended upon Houston. When the fighting was done, seventeen people were dead, including four policemen and two soldiers. Sixteen others were wounded. The federal response to the soldiers' actions was swift and merciless. By conservative estimates, 103 soldiers were tried, 100 court-martialed, 13 of them hanged, and 41 sentenced to life imprisonment.[16]

Brutality, hostility, grave injustice, and isolation—Barbara Jordan's grandparents and parents experienced them all. Surely they remembered the more hopeful experience of African Americans during Reconstruction. That recent past could have seemed only brighter. Perhaps they knew of a more distant history of blacks among the Spanish and Mexicans, when many people of African heritage were not free but freer. Yet Jordan's family and neighbors in the black wards wanted more than the return to a freer time; they wanted a future of still greater freedom and opportunity, equal to that of all people in the United States. For Barbara Jordan, who proclaimed herself a symbol of African American progress on the stage of the 1976 Democratic Convention, this was the history that preceded her. She was born into it on February 21, 1936, in the midst of the Great Depression.

3 Three Bicycles and a Bed

Barbara Jordan grew up in a brick house on Sharon Street in the Fourth Ward, northeast of downtown Houston. There she lived with three generations of the Jordan family: her mother Arlyne, her father Ben, her older sisters Rose Mary and Bennie, and her grandfather and step-grandmother, Charles Jordan and Alice Reed Jordan. The Jordan home was on a block of houses with small, neatly kept backyards, fenced and filled with juniper, mulberry, and oleander trees, and front lawns decorated with hedges and shrubs. The street was paved. Barbara Jordan's home had electricity, gas, and plumbing.[1] In the Jordan household, a room was something to be shared, a bed someplace to lie on with others. Barbara's grandparents slept in the front bedroom. Her parents had the small bedroom in the back. She and her sisters slept together on a fold-out bed.

For most African Americans in Houston, this house and neighborhood was strikingly different from the wooden buildings, outhouse privies, and unpaved streets that they knew as home. Barbara's father and her grandfather had bought the home together. The Jordan men, her father Ben in particular, dominated the household, including Barbara, when she was at home. Ben Jordan was a formidable presence, a stern and religious man, charismatic and handsome as well. He had grown up in Edna, Texas, where he had been a football star and a bright student. After high school, he attended on scholarship the famous Tuskegee Institute in Alabama, founded by Booker T. Washington, the most powerful African American leader in the late nineteenth century. The Tuskegee Institute practiced what Washington had advocated in his famous "Atlanta Compromise" speech of 1895. Faced with a violent backlash against African Americans throughout the South, Washington proposed that if hostile whites would leave African Americans to live in peace, African Americans would not pursue social equality with white Americans. They would not try to fight against voting restrictions in the South. They would pursue decent but less than ambitious jobs, in fields that did not require higher education. (Tuskegee gave its students what came to be known as a vocational education.) Above all else, African Americans would show the rest of America they could be respected members of society, willing to live in peace but segregated from whites. Raising his hand, Washington said that whites and blacks might live together but separate, as naturally as the fingers on his hand.[2]

Ben Jordan did not believe in segregation, but he believed strongly that it was important for African Americans to show their high morals and good manners, which he learned at home and at Tuskegee. Like

The Jordan sisters, from left to right: Bennie,
Barbara, and Rose Mary

Booker T. Washington, he believed such respectability would have a political effect, for if African Americans were to be upstanding members of society, they would show that stereotypes of blacks were simply false. African Americans were not lazy or unintelligent or easily attracted to crime and other forms of sinning. By being respectable, they could make it difficult for white people to have such bigoted ideas about African Americans.

Ben Jordan attended Tuskegee until his senior year, when money became a problem and his mother fell ill. He then returned to Houston, where he got a job at the Houston Terminal Warehouse and Cold Storage.[3] He saved his money and joined the Good Hope Missionary Baptist Church. His father was chairman of the deacon board at Good Hope. Eventually Ben Jordan became a deacon. When his mother died, Ben Jordan and his father used the insurance money from her death and the help of President Franklin Delano Roosevelt's New Deal (government programs designed to help Americans during the Depression) to buy the home on Sharon Street. Two years later, Charles Jordan married Alice Reed, an English teacher, piano teacher, and prominent member of Good Hope.[4] A year after his father's marriage, Ben Jordan himself married Arlyne Patten, a choir member and talented speaker at Good Hope. To Barbara, her mother was "the speaker de luxe. She was the most eloquent, articulate person I ever heard; if she'd been a man she would have been a preacher." In the Jordan home, however, Arlyne became a housewife, an occasional "day worker"—a maid—and eventually a mother. She prepared the meals, washed the clothes, and looked after the household while her husband and in-laws worked. Then she had children, first

Rose Mary, then Bennie, and finally Barbara Charline Jordan, Barbara's middle name honoring her grandfather Charles Jordan.[5]

Religion and the Good Hope Missionary Baptist Church were a dominant feature of the household Barbara knew as a child—religion as interpreted by her father. From the end of the Civil War onward, when all-black churches could organize freely in Texas, the black church was one of the mainstays of the black community, keeping its people together amidst the sufferings of segregation and discrimination. Since nearly all African Americans belonged to a church, the black churches often acted as a means of spreading the news in the days before African American newspapers were established. They occasionally functioned like a credit union since there were no African American banks; and at a time when the court system was heavily prejudiced against African Americans or uninterested in them, the black churches sometimes acted as a community court for resolving disputes.[6] Good Hope was just such an institution in Houston, a long-standing part of the African American community. Good Hope supported the Jordans, and in turn the Jordans supported Good Hope. For the Jordans to belong to Good Hope was also to live by the principles of the Baptist religion. On Sundays before attending church, Charles and Ben Jordan would test the girls' knowledge of the Bible. Ben Jordan liked his daughters to go to Sunday school and church in the morning, as well as afternoon services or Bible classes.[7] Barbara's father showed his love for his children through the demands that he placed upon them to be respected and ambitious. He never hit his children, but his voice and authority commanded. He wanted all of them to work hard and to achieve much. When Barbara would bring home report cards with all As and one B, he would ask her why she got a B.[8] From her father, Barbara Jordan learned to be fiercely demanding of herself and to be a hard worker. You must strive to better yourself, he taught Barbara, but you should expect that nobody will give you anything. You'll have to work hard to get someplace.

Ben Jordan wanted his three daughters to be raised alike and according to the rules of his religion. When Barbara awoke each morning, there were her sisters in the same bed, living by the same rules. As Barbara grew older, she believed deeply in single standards. As a lawyer, she believed that everyone should be treated the same under the law. Barbara absorbed and admired Ben Jordan's convictions.

But Barbara also felt her life was too strictly confined when she was under her father's roof. She felt everyone should be required to follow the same principles, but there could be too many rules. Even if everyone followed the same principles—well, that did not mean one person's wishes should dictate all those rules. Ben Jordan controlled the money in the household, and his decisions about where to spend it determined what clothes Barbara wore and what food she ate. He made sure that Barbara knew that. When Barbara wanted to have meat with meals, Ben was often against it and flatly told his daughter, "If you want some meat, you can go buy it." As Barbara and her sisters grew older, Ben Jordan liked to brag, "I'm raising three girls in the heart of the city. And they don't drink, they don't smoke, they don't dance, they don't play cards, they don't go to the movies." Barbara loved her father, but she thought he was too proud of his rules. She felt that if she and her sisters had followed those rules strictly, they would have a been a bunch of "freaks."[9]

There were differences among the three girls, and for Barbara, her difference could be traced to the influence of her other grandfather. Barbara Jordan's childhood was split between the world of her father and the world of her mother's father, John Edward Patten. Every Sunday, after morning services, Barbara's family would have a big meal at Grandmother and Grandfather Patten's house. Then, when it came time for afternoon services or Bible classes, Rose Mary and Bennie would want to go back to church. But not Barbara. "You don't have to," her grandfather Patten would say.[10]

Instead Barbara would stay with her grandfather Patten, who unlike his wife and daughter, refused to set foot in Good Hope or any other church. Barbara's grandfather Patten was fiercely independent and passionately devoted to his youngest granddaughter. He ran a junkyard in the Fourth Ward, near downtown, from which he would sell scrap iron, paper, rags, and manure. He collected the junk with a wagon and two mules that he owned. Once in a while, city inspectors came by and complained about the mules and manure so near to the center of Houston. "Clean it up," they would tell him. Grandfather Patten would respond, "Of course I'll clean it up." But he wasn't one to be ordered around by white people. He'd take scrap tin and cardboard and construct a kind of fence, so that a passerby couldn't see the mules and manure so well. Then he'd go about his business as usual.

On those Sundays, Barbara worked alongside him in the junkyard, heaping the metal into piles, collecting the rags, and stacking the paper. The manure was shoveled into baskets and sold as fertilizer. For all this, Grandfather Patten paid her a part of the day's proceeds and got her a money belt to keep her earnings in, so Barbara actually had spending money as a child.[11]

But that was only the beginning of the day. Next, Grandfather Patten would walk to Matt Garner's barbecue restaurant, where no blacks were allowed in. There, at the back door, he would be handed a free bag of "reg'lars," the ends of ribs and sausages that got left off in the preparation of the customers' meals. Left off or not, reg'lars were fine eating. Back at the junkyard, Grandfather Patten would share the pile of steaming hot meat covered in barbeque sauce with Barbara. Then they would talk.[12]

Talking with Grandfather Patten was unlike any other talking Barbara did with adults during her childhood. Barbara felt that most adults didn't speak with her when they talked. They just set down rules for her or asked her to repeat the rules out loud until they were satisfied she understood them. With Grandfather Patten, she felt listened to and accepted. She opened up to him. In turn, he taught her to see the world as a place for constant education and improvement. Don't be like other folk, he would tell Barbara. Go your own way. The education she got from him lasted her entire life.

Even if he did not set foot in churches, Grandfather Patten was a religious man. In fact he thought of himself as a true Christian. Grandfather Patten would read portions of the Bible to Barbara and then interpret them for her. The lessons were clear and focused, but they had an individual twist peculiar to Grandfather Patten—to a story from the Bible he would add something from his own experience. If you want to be a true

Barbara's grandfather, John Edward Patten

Christian, he told Barbara, then do as I tell you. Love people, but don't trust them. Be sure to realize you are different from everybody else. You'll have to fight to stay independent. If you don't watch out, you'll be thrown off course and end up like everybody else.[13]

Grandpa Patten's house was unlike the middle-class Jordan household. He and his wife, Martha Ann Fletcher Patten, rented their home, a wooden house without trees or grass in front. Barbara would help her grandparents sweep the yard to keep it clean. The Patten home was without electricity or plumbing. When they needed water, they used a faucet out back. Their bathroom was an outhouse. If they needed to iron clothing, they heated a solid metal iron on a wood stove.[14]

Those were the physical differences from Barbara's home on Sharon Street, but there were other, more important differences. From the lessons he taught to the way he behaved with others, John Ed Patten showed Barbara that he had known suffering, misery, and injustice. He had come from an accomplished family. One relative, Thelma Patten, was the first black woman doctor in Houston.[15] She had delivered Barbara in the Jordan home. By some accounts, John Ed Patten's father was a lawyer in Washington, D.C. He had been one of the last African Americans elected to the Texas House of Representatives during Reconstruction.[16]

John Ed Patten also knew disappointment and tragedy. His grandfather, he was told, was killed by a white man. His father had abandoned the family when John Ed was young. Barbara Jordan's grandfather and his brother grew up with their mother, a stepfather and six half-brothers and sisters in the community of Ever-green, east of Houston. When John Ed was a teenager, his brother, Steve, died in a mysterious accident while visiting a blacksmith shop with his horse. Someone tried to take the horse from him, but Steve fought back. During the fight, Steve was shot through the heart.[17]

For all the sadness Grandfather Patten knew as a child and young man, the defining event of his adult life was the result of racial injustice. Once grown up, John Ed Patten moved to Houston. Married and with three children—Arlyne, Johnnie, and the infant Ed—he owned a candy store on San Felipe Street in the business district of the Fourth Ward. He worked hard at that business, and it began to grow. Then, one night in May 1918, as he was closing up shop, a man entered the store, snatched cash from the open till, and fled out the door. Furious, John Ed Patten grabbed his gun and chased after him. When the thief ran into a busy restaurant, John Ed followed after him. Inside, Grandfather Patten lost him but decided the thief had run out of the restaurant. At the door of the café, pistol in hand, John Ed Patten paused a moment—long enough to be well noticed by the customers—and then continued across the street into the dark. Suddenly he heard people chasing after him and a voice crying out, "Catch that nigger; he has a gun."[18] Then he heard the sound of someone shooting at him.

Although chasing a thief, Grandfather Patten had suddenly become a potential criminal and a menace to white people—a black man with a gun. Grandfather Patten knew he was in danger, and he began to run. He fled through the darkness of the Fourth Ward. At the end of two blocks, terrified, John Ed Patten stopped and threw his hands up in surrender. Someone shot him through the open palm of one hand. As he recalled the event later, he was so frightened that he did not remember shooting back in self-defense. But he had done so. His pursuers, he soon found out, were the police, and one of them was wounded.

John Ed Patten was brought before a grand jury and indicted for "assault with intent to murder." Then came his court trial, which unleashed the fear, anger, and racial prejudice of white Houston upon him. His trial began less than one year after the Camp Logan race riot; the police and all other whites in Houston had fresh memories of what black soldiers had done to them. So the incident was judged not as a conflict between people but as an example of unacceptable rebellion against white authority. A black man had shot at white police officers and wounded one of them. The wounded officer declared that Grandfather Patten had threatened him, declaring "Stop, you white son-of-a-bitch." He said that "this darky" had tried to shoot him six times.[19]

John Ed Patten tried to explain why he had a gun: It was dark and the people chasing him had not identified themselves as policemen. The officers had only said "catch that nigger," which frightened him. His lawyer observed that John Ed Patten had been shot in the palm, clear evidence that he had been trying to surrender when he was shot at. His firing of his gun in return was self-defense against unknown attackers.[20] White storekeepers who knew him testified on behalf of Patten. But it was no use. The judge did not instruct the jury to consider self-defense. The all-white jury convicted him, and in February 1919, after a fruitless appeal, John Ed Patten was sent to Huntsville State Penitentiary to serve a ten-year sentence.[21]

Huntsville Prison was a horror. Prisoners lived in rat- and roach-infested cells. They worked the nearby fields every day, shackled to each other with metal chokers around their necks. Guards routinely whipped them until they bled. While he was in prison, his family deprived of money, his younger son, Ed, died of malnutrition. Six years later, Grandfather Patten was pardoned for his crime by Governor Miriam "Ma" Ferguson, but the damage was done. He could not forget the horror of that experience. Grandfather Patten returned to a world that he now distrusted. The racial injustice he had suffered found its way indirectly into nearly all aspects of his behavior. He wasn't interested in church life. He mistrusted people even as he tried to love them.[22]

John Ed Patten opened his junk business and devoted himself to work and to loving his daughter Arlyne, Barbara's mother. He encouraged Arlyne to educate herself, to be independent, and to become the fine speaker she eventually became at the Good Hope Missionary Baptist Church. He had ambitions for her. Then, to his disappointment, Arlyne became a housewife and mother, a supporter of her middle-class husband rather than a success on her own. John Ed Patten refused to attend his daughter's wedding.[23]

At the birth of his third granddaughter, Barbara Charline Jordan, John Ed Patten suddenly changed. He was no longer a disappointed, lonely man but a man on a mission: to make his granddaughter into the kind of person he wished Arlyne had been. Everywhere he went, he carried photographs of Barbara with him. On the back of one photo, he wrote out in capital letters "MY HEART." On the back of another, he wrote out Barbara's middle name as "Edine" rather than Charline, to honor his feeling that Barbara descended from him rather than Charles Jordan. As Barbara Jordan grew up, he encouraged her independence. He told Barbara, "Don't ever marry, and don't work for anybody except yourself." Be different, he told her.[25]

On their Sundays together, Grandfather Patten repeatedly told Barbara Jordan she was special. Once, when she was still a little girl, he gave her diamond earrings. Another time, Barbara asked him for a bicycle. He found her a bike while he was on his rounds collecting junk. Barbara Jordan was thrilled with the gift, but soon she wanted a new bike. He bought her a blue-and-white Schwinn. Later, he found another bike on a collecting trip. At one time, Barbara had three bicycles.[26] The bed at the Jordan home may have been a sign of the single standard under which all should live in Ben Jordan's household. But the bicycles were their own sign to Barbara Jordan. They were a sign of Grandfather Patten's astonishing love for her and of his singular message: Be an individual. Don't trust anyone too much, but love everyone. Rely only on yourself; you'll need to maintain your privacy to do so. The message and the memories lasted with Barbara Jordan. Like her grandfather, she fiercely valued independence, and she guarded her privacy carefully. Throughout her life, she carried pictures of John Ed Patten in her wallet.[27]

4 A Spirited Girl

As she grew into her teens and approached high school, Barbara Jordan became the independent person her Grandfather Patten encouraged her to be. Her two sisters made it easier for Barbara to be a little less restricted and a little less supervised by their father. Their influence also made Ben Jordan a little more supportive of his youngest daughter, even if he found Barbara to be a handful.

Rose Mary attracted the most attention from Ben Jordan. The oldest girl, she had grown up aware that she had to please her father. Rose Mary also felt genuinely punished if she disappointed him. She learned from her father and became increasingly attached to him. She loved Good Hope, and as she grew up, she had strong religious beliefs. On Sunday mornings, Rose Mary would often volunteer to read scripture to the family. At Good Hope, she participated in Bible drills, the Baptist Young People's Union, and vacation Bible school.

Rose Mary gave Ben Jordan little reason to feel concerned about her. She rarely rebelled. Yet Ben Jordan continued to watch her carefully throughout her teenage years. Tall and attractive, Rose Mary was allowed to begin dating in high school. Ben Jordan gave her a curfew time but refused to give her a door key: She would have to knock when she returned home, so he knew exactly when she came in the door. Then he could smell for any liquor on her breath or smoke on her clothes.[1]

Ben Jordan watched over his daughter carefully because he not only loved her but needed her to be successful. Many people said that Ben Jordan identified with his daughter, a powerful reason why he so carefully raised Rose Mary. Ben Jordan was a respected member of his community and had achieved a modest financial stability, yet he felt dissatisfied. In spite of his intelligence and ambition, he had not graduated from Tuskegee. He often felt frustrated that his industrial education had not allowed him to enter a white-collar, professional field. Throughout his life, he struggled for ways to improve his lot beyond the union job he held at Houston Terminal Warehouse and Cold Storage. He vowed that his daughters would achieve what he hadn't. He had been a good student, so he expected Rose Mary to get all As in school. After high school, he expected Rose Mary to go on with her education, to graduate from a college, and then to have a fine job as a professional. Rose Mary seemed more than willing to pursue those goals.[2]

Because Rose Mary was her father's favorite, Bennie could be different. Like Rose Mary, Bennie had been a penny-collection girl at church when she was young. But outside of Good Hope, she did not seek her father's approval the way her older sister did. While her father was constantly telling them what they could not do, she was drawn to anything that brought warmth and pleasure within their home. Often she found that among the women of the household. Before those Sunday meals at Grandmother and Grandfather Patten's home, she loved to perch herself on a stool in the kitchen and lick the left-over cake batter off the metal mixing spoon.[3] When she thought of her home life, she thought of music. Their Sharon Street household had a piano, which her step-grandmother, Alice Reed Jordan, would play while the family stood around it and sang. As a teenager, she began to study music seriously under the watchful eye of her step-aunt Mamie Reed, Alice Reed Jordan's daughter, who was often at their house. To Bennie, Mamie was no average aunt. She was smart and accomplished, a music teacher at Phillis Wheatley High School, which the girls eventually attended. Mamie had studied voice at Prairie View College in Texas, Westminster Choir College in Princeton, New Jersey, and the University of Iowa. She had taken voice workshops at Columbia University in New York and at the Fred Waring Clinic in Pennsylvania.[4] From Mamie, Bennie learned to love music. She continued to sing in the Good Hope choir throughout high school and college. She also learned another, more abstract lesson from Mamie: It was important to have someone older to guide her, someone whom she believed accepted her without qualification.

In turn, Bennie acted as a constant companion and protector to Barbara. Rose Mary loved her youngest sister; Bennie adored and befriended her. When Barbara was young, Bennie convinced Rose Mary to let Barbara sleep in the middle of their bed, Barbara's favorite position. She washed the dishes for Barbara when it was her little sister's chore. She counseled Barbara on how to cope with school and how to make friends. As they grew older, and the age differences between them lessened, Bennie became good friends with Barbara.

For Barbara, the rules of Ben Jordan's household were the same, but Rose Mary had absorbed some of her father's attention, and Bennie had set a precedent for being different. Her two older sisters provided her with the experience and advice that allowed her to be as independent as she could.

And Barbara was different. At school, she told jokes, passed notes, and laughed out loud when the teacher expected silence.[6] In church, she was relatively uninterested. In the neighborhood, she was a bold leader among a gang of friends. From early childhood, she was a big, assertive personality. At home, she was spanked often enough that she'd learned how to pull in her buttocks so the leather belt didn't hurt much.[7] Physically, she towered over not only most girls but also most boys (at least until high school)—which only made her booming voice and independent ways all the more apparent.

At the age of ten, she showed her independence in an unlikely way. She joined Good Hope officially by declaring herself ready to be baptized. This was strange. For Barbara, religion offered little joy. She later said that church taught her how to die but not how to live.[8] Her decision to join Good Hope at the age of ten had nothing to do with religion, however. Before she was baptized, her sisters and friends had insisted that she could play only the role of "sinner" in one of their favorite neighborhood games, "Christians and sinners."

Jordan with the congregation of the Good Hope Missionary Baptist Church

She got tired of that, so without telling her parents, she decided to do something about it.

During church services, when the Reverend Albert Lucas made his usual call for new members to be baptized, ten-year-old Barbara quickly rose. Until that time, Barbara's practice was to fall asleep as soon as the Reverend Mr. Lucas began to speak, her head resting on her mother's lap. Now, Arlyne Jordan watched with astonishment as her youngest daughter popped up and strode quickly down the aisle of the church. "Where is she going?" Arlyne said aloud. Seated at the front of the church, Deacons Ben and Charles Jordan smiled broadly. They took this to be a sign of Barbara seeing the light; at only ten years of age, she had found her way to Jesus Christ. They beamed with pride as Barbara took the Reverend Mr. Lucas's hand. But Ben and Charles Jordan misunderstood her motives. Barbara continued to feel an independence from religion that John Ed Patten had nurtured. She had acted only to make a neighborhood game more fun for herself.[9]

Above all else, Barbara was strong-willed, and she needed to declare her wishes. It was part of her style. For two years, under the orders of her parents, she took piano lessons from Mattie Thomas of the Au Fait music school. Then, at age eleven, she decided she didn't want to anymore, so she waited for the next class and before all the other students, she declared to her teacher that she "no longer wished to take piano." Embarrassed, Mattie Thomas called Ben Jordan to report that Barbara was a little too outspoken in her ways.[10]

Ben Jordan wasn't pleased, but he wasn't surprised. On other occasions, Barbara openly confronted her father. Barbara decided she wanted a particular warm coat with a hood on it, but Ben Jordan refused to buy it; the coat was too expensive, he said. Not to be denied, Barbara asked her Grandfather Patten, who bought her the coat. Some time later, Ben Jordan showed off the coat to a friend as Barbara wore it. Pointing to it, he said, "It's beautiful, isn't it?" Barbara shot back, "You didn't buy it for me."[11]

Barbara's mother rarely protested about her husband's control of her life, but her displeasure and her defiance appeared, too. She decided on her own that three children were enough for her to care for, so she decided to take charge of her body. She bussed to the

Arlyne Jordan, Barbara's mother, in front of the Campbell Street house

Planned Parenthood Center downtown and secured birth control.[12] She secretly arranged for the girls to go to a Shirley Temple movie that Ben Jordan had forbidden them to see.[13] On one and only one occasion she raised her voice to Ben Jordan. She demanded that he pay to dry-clean their Sunday clothes, which she had hand-made out of gabardine. Exceptional as they were, these tiny acts of rebellion were noticed by Barbara. It may be that Barbara sensed her mother's frustration with Ben Jordan and expressed it herself. Barbara could not openly defy her father. In general she did as he told her. But she needed to resist her father as well, and that feeling soon increased.[14]

In 1949, when Barbara was thirteen years old, Ben Jordan made a change that strongly affected all the Jordans. He decided that he had been "called to preach." He accepted a position as the pastor at the Greater Pleasant Hill Baptist Church in nearby Houston Heights, all the while continuing his job at Houston Warehouse and Storage.[15] Naturally, he expected his family to participate in the life of his new church. Arlyne, Rose Mary, Bennie, and Barbara moved away from the community of Good Hope, from their connections with friends they had known for decades and even from the elder Jordans, to be the first family of Ben Jordan's new church. The Sunday afternoon meals with the Pattens ended, too. To Barbara and her sisters, it felt as though they had moved countries away. Rose Mary cried the day they stopped going to Good Hope. Her time at the new church was mercifully brief. In the fall, she left for Prairie View College to study music education.[16]

what she wanted. Barbara learned from her father how to work hard and to discipline herself so that she could pursue her own ambitions. She was still a teenager at heart and in spirit; she continued to resist the authority of her father, as she would well into adulthood. But she had learned how to maneuver around him and how to find value from his control of her life—lessons that would prove useful in the political world she would face as an adult.

5 Gaining Direction

At the beginning of high school, Barbara Jordan was adventuresome, free-spirited, even reckless; she was distracted from her education. By its end, she found a calling. Barbara attended Phillis Wheatley High School in the Fifth Ward of Houston, one of two relatively new high schools for African Americans. It was established in the 1920s and offered Houston blacks, for the first time, a standardized high school curriculum.[1] The name of the school itself indicated its pioneering status. A freed slave who was born around 1753 and died in 1784, Phillis Wheatley was the first African American to publish a volume of poetry, in 1773.[2] Barbara became a pioneer herself; but nothing about her start would have led anyone to predict that. She was too busy enjoying her newfound freedom.

From the first moment of high school, Barbara Jordan felt liberated. Even if there were rules to be followed, she wasn't under the supervision of her father at home, and she wasn't confined to a pew in church.

ned according to Act of Parliament, Sept. 1. 1773 by Arch. Bell, Bookseller N° 8 near the Saracens Head Aldgate.

P O E M S

ON

VARIOUS SUBJECTS,

RELIGIOUS AND MORAL.

BY

PHILLIS WHEATLEY,

NEGRO SERVANT to Mr. JOHN WHEATLEY, of BOSTON, in NEW ENGLAND.

L O N D O N:

Printed for A. BELL, Bookseller, Aldgate; and sold by Meſſrs. COX and BERRY, King-Street, *BOSTON.*

M DCC LXXIII.

The title page of Phillis Wheatley's Poems on Various Subjects. *It is remarkable that Wheatley was published and wonderful that her poems were well received.*

Her first priority was not to study but to explore the opportunities surrounding school and to establish a group of friends. At the football games, especially the Thanksgiving Day game with archrival Jack Yates High School in the Third Ward, Barbara was one of the most vocal supporters of the team. She was convinced that she led the cheers better than the cheerleaders.[3]

Soon she developed a circle of friends with a routine all their own. Evelyn and Mary Elizabeth Justice, Charles White, and her sister Bennie were always in the group, but in total there were ten or twelve of them who would gather after school. Often, within a few blocks of Wheatley, they would stop for hamburgers, hot dogs, and drinks. Barbara and Charles White would pay because they had money. Then they would begin the hour-long walk home to Campbell Street. At Solo Street, shortly before home, they would string themselves across the width of the road, all ten to twelve of them, so nothing could pass—not even a bicycle. Then they would slowly walk the final distance.[4] They were testing the limits of their own boldness. They were seeing what they could get away with.

Barbara assumed the role of leader among her group of friends. In those days, one could get a driver's license in Texas at the age of fourteen. Leaping at the opportunity, Barbara took driver's education at Wheatley and got her license. In the evenings, she would borrow her father's dark-blue Oldsmobile to drive her gang of friends to the drive-in for food. Occasionally on weekends, Barbara organized slumber parties, at which Bennie, the Justice sisters, and she stayed up all night talking about sex and boys.[5]

Her new freedom seemed to make her impatient. She wanted new experiences. She wanted everything immediately, and she wanted everything faster. No longer satisfied with the speed of her bicycle, she asked Grandfather Patten to hook up a motor to her Schwinn. At Grandfather Patten's request, she researched the matter and discovered that it would take $300 worth of reinforcements to motorize her bicycle. He seemed willing to do it. But Arlyne killed the plan: Her daughter was not going to be flying along the road, with her skirt raised immodestly by the wind.[6]

A motorized bike signified one impulse Barbara Jordan had at the time: to be wild and carefree, to throw caution to the wind. Who cares about a skirt flying up? Her other impulse was to be like the other teenage girls. She cut her hair in a pageboy bob and wore what everyone else did: bobby socks, rhinestone jewelry, scoop-necked dresses, and earrings. She read *Seventeen* magazine and liked "loud-colored" shoes.[7]

In spite of all her attempts to be like the other girls, Barbara was different. There was her size: at 5 feet 8 inches and 175 pounds, she was big.[8] She also exuded strength and intelligence. She was a force among people, her booming voice capturing attention and commanding respect. It helped fuel her belief that she was a leader. Not everything about her physical appearance, however, was well received at her high school. Barbara Jordan had beautiful, dark black skin, but her color led to one of her first memorable experiences with race prejudice. It came at the hands of fellow African Americans. At Wheatley, Barbara found that the lighter a student's skin and the straighter a student's hair, the more popular the student. The lighter, straight-haired girls had the best chance of being elected "Miss Wheatley"—student representative of the school—or one of Miss Wheatley's attendants.[9]

Phillis Wheatley High School

Because of this favoritism, Barbara Jordan knew that she would also not be selected a cheerleader even if she cheered better than those on the squad. Barbara felt this bias from schoolteachers as well, one of whom she called "color-struck" because the teacher preferred students whose hair didn't require straightening creams.[10]

None of these prejudices was a surprise to Barbara's father. Ben Jordan clearly recognized that skin color made a difference in that era. At Barbara's birth, one of his first remarks was "Why is she so dark?" His reaction may have signaled his surprise because both he and his wife were relatively light-skinned. Or it may have been a sign that he wished she were lighter. In any case, Ben Jordan knew that Barbara's life was going to be harder because of the darker complexion of her skin.

Explaining this favoritism is not easy. Was it a common form of bigotry, that African Americans were less attractive than whites? Was it that African Americans had come to believe that the whiter one appeared, the more successful one could be? Many traced the behavior to a status system that existed during slavery, which favored lighter-skinned house servants over the darker field hands. But it continued in the twentieth century.

Barbara's reaction to this situation at Wheatley was to accept it reluctantly but to minimize its effects upon her life. She clearly objected to the bias. She did not like "color-struck" teachers, and she felt as if "the world had decided that we were all Negro, but that some of us were more Negro than others."[12] Her style, however, was not to protest but to steer around direct confrontation. She would tolerate the limitations for now, but she would certainly never be ashamed of the color of her skin. While some of her classmates used bleaching creams to lighten their skin, she would never try to change her color.

In general, Barbara Jordan wasn't focused on race matters. She was preoccupied with being a teenager, figuring out what to do in high school. Of course, she remembered the experience of her grandfather, and she was aware that her world was a world of African Americans; whites lived and worked elsewhere. But she did not appear to have feared whites or to have felt the insult and the humiliation that African American adults regularly experienced. She lived among African Americans and shopped mostly in stores run by African Americans. She did not regularly see the greater wealth of white people or the better schools white children attended. She walked or drove places, so she rarely rode the bus, where she might have continually seen the effects of segregation.[13]

She was certainly aware of segregation. She recalled the separate drinking fountains for whites and blacks when, as a little girl, she went with her mother to a department store in downtown Houston to shop. She knew that in the downtown area there were fewer bathrooms for black people than for whites. She called downtown Houston a "totally white world." It didn't feel "right" for blacks and whites to be separated, she said.[14]

But segregation would be around for a long time, she thought, so it was more constructive to focus on bettering herself. In her notes for a high school speech on integration, she wrote, "let it be realized by every student that the challenge facing us is not the defense of any system, be it segregated or integrated; the challenge facing us is to equip ourselves that we will be able to take our place wherever we are in the affairs of men."[15] Barbara Jordan experienced the great divide between black and white; but it was not yet something that outraged her. Instead, her personal goals were her focus. She and her Grandfather Patten believed that she was special and different, but she decided that she would have to be special and different among black people only.[16]

In spite of her independent ways, Barbara Jordan was following her father in this regard. With Ben Jordan's guidance, the Jordan family adjusted and reluctantly accepted the limitations they saw around them. Segregation and racism did not seem to be actively discussed in the Jordan home, nor were the Jordans politically active in the advancing civil-rights movement. Instead the Jordans focused on making successes of themselves. That in itself, they believed, would show the potential of African Americans.[17]

Nonetheless, the first signs of the dismantling of segregation had already appeared, and a political movement was under way. On July 26, 1948, one year before Barbara entered high school, President Harry S. Truman signed an executive order to end segregation in the armed forces. That same year, a Truman commission called for new consideration of "civil rights"—one of the first times this phrase had been used. Jackie Robinson broke the color line in baseball when he began playing for the Brooklyn Dodgers in 1947, as did the great Negro League pitcher Satchel Paige, when he began playing for Cleveland the following year.[18] Amidst these changes, in 1949, Barbara Jordan entered high school.

While the Jordans tolerated things as they were, many of their friends and neighbors had begun to organize themselves against segregation. Twice during the 1940s, when Barbara Jordan was a child, the Good Hope Church was at the center of African American civil-rights activism in Houston; and at moments, court cases that originated in Houston were at the center of antisegregation efforts in the nation. Within Good Hope, the leader of these efforts was none other than the Reverend Albert Lucas himself. Lucas had helped organize the Texas State Conference of Branches of the National Association for the Advancement of Colored People (NAACP), and in 1940 he was state president of the NAACP, the most powerful civil-rights organization in the country.[19]

Led by their Legal Defense Fund attorney, Thurgood Marshall, the NAACP chose two court cases from Houston as part of their efforts to dismantle segregation.[20] In 1940—the year Reverend Albert Lucas was state president of the NAACP—Marshall filed suit in federal court on behalf of Dr. Lonnie Smith, a Good Hope congregation member. Smith, Marshall and others wanted to eliminate the all-white primary elections by which the Democratic party in Texas nominated its candidates. Because nearly all Texans were Democrats at the time, to win the primary was effectively to win the general election. Yet African Americans were not allowed to vote in the primary. Thurgood Marshall argued that the Democrats' excluding of blacks from the primaries violated the Fifteenth Amendment of the Constitution, the post-Civil War Amendment that among other things, guaranteed all Americans the right to vote, regardless of race. In 1944 the Supreme Court ruled in *Smith* v. *Allwright* that Marshall and the NAACP were right.[21]

Two years later, Marshall filed another suit in Houston, asking the courts to strike down segregation in higher education. Heman Sweatt, a Houston resident, was denied permission to attend the University of Texas law school in Austin because he was black. There was no law school in Texas that admitted blacks,

Thurgood Marshall (standing), Charles Houston (center), and Donald Gaines Murray prepare a desegregation case against the University of Maryland in 1935.

so Marshall insisted that segregation denied Sweatt equal opportunity. In spite of what the Supreme Court had ruled in the 1896 case of *Plessy* v. *Ferguson*, Marshall argued, separate was not equal. But in 1950—when Barbara Jordan was in high school—the United

States Supreme Court ruled in *Sweatt* v. *Painter* that separate could still be equal. If there was no other law school, Heman Sweatt must be admitted to the University of Texas Law School. But if another law school were to open for African Americans, then segregation could remain. Firmly dedicated to maintaining segregation, the state of Texas quickly established a law school at Texas State University for Negroes in Houston.[22]

These court cases and the fight against segregation were actively part of the discussions at Good Hope during Barbara Jordan's childhood and adolescence. The Reverend Lucas insisted that Good Hope combine religion and civil rights: "Prayer without action isn't worth a dip of Scott's snuff," he said.[23] Middle-class African Americans in Houston were distinctly impatient with segregation. Through such court actions, they politely but clearly demanded change. Yet the Jordan family, although against segregation, did not appear to be especially active or interested in the civil-rights movement.

Barbara Jordan had more immediate and personal interests. Within a short time in high school, Barbara's intelligence and leadership abilities became apparent to her. She didn't study much, but several teachers noticed how bright she was. Sometimes her intelligence appeared in less than tactful ways. On one occasion, she upstaged a science teacher during a lesson, correcting the teacher before the rest of the class. The teacher told Barbara's Aunt Mamie, who suggested Barbara change her ways so that Mamie would not have to tell her father.[24] That was enough reason for Barbara to become less outspoken, but she had another reason. She had decided that for college, she preferred to stay in Houston and attend Texas State University for Negroes, recently renamed Texas Southern. To do so, she needed both good grades and a good record of achievements.

In a short time she showed that she was not simply ambitious but calculating and savvy. When the dean of the girl students, Evelyn Cunningham, suggested that Barbara run for class attendant, Barbara's response was matter-of-fact and practical: "Miss Cunningham, I am not the right light color, and I don't have the clothes, the whole thing." Evelyn Cunningham disagreed. She thought Barbara was both smart and popular. But Barbara believed that she knew better. Instead, she set her sights on becoming Girl of the Year, an award from a national black sorority for the outstanding girl in the senior class, based solely on record.[25]

For more than a year, without telling her friends, she planned and acted on a strategy to win selection as Girl of the Year. It was a sign that she was becoming shrewd and political. She dedicated herself toward clubs and activities that would help her cause. She sang with the Wheatley Lovable Troubadours. She became a member of the honor society. Most importantly, she became a member of the debate team, where she was wildly successful.[26]

To no surprise, public speaking came easily to Barbara. She had learned to memorize and to recite poetry and prayers while at Greater Pleasant Hill. She came from a family that insisted she speak clearly and that valued public speech. In spite of her objection to church, it had exposed Barbara Jordan to a powerful tradition of oratory, the sermons that the Reverend Mr.

Lucas and her father gave every week. Like all sermons, their speeches were designed to inspire and to persuade an audience. Yet they were also practicing a distinct art form, a centuries-old tradition whose roots were in the black churches of the North and South and in black spiritual music. Each sermon was like a carefully composed piece of music, with recognizable rhythms, variations in volume, pace, and dramatic emphasis. This very tradition is part of what made the writing and speaking of ministers such as Mordecai Johnson, Howard Thurman, and Martin Luther King Jr. so beautiful and powerful.

Barbara also realized that her voice gave her an additional advantage. She was quickly successful at debate and quickly noticed. When the sponsor of the declamation oratorical contests at Wheatley heard her, he immediately asked her to compete for Wheatley against other schools. Barbara was almost instantly a success. She began traveling to local, regional, and district contests, where she consistently won, and she made it to the state finals at Prairie View College each year that she competed.

In 1952 she was named Girl of the Year, yet her successes at speaking soon overshadowed the importance of that award for her. Through church, she received her greatest recognition as a speaker. At a statewide meet in Waco, she won first prize in the Baptist Ushers Oratorical Contest—$50 and a trip to the national competition in Chicago for a speech entitled "Is the Necessity for a Higher Education More in Demand Today Than a Decade Ago?" It was her first trip out of the segregated South and away from the protected environment of home and neighborhood. Riding the train with her mother, she glimpsed a larger world out there, full of

Barbara Jordan winning first place in an oratorical contest in Chicago, Illinois

potential and adventure for a sixteen-year-old. Then, in Chicago, one of the few girls in the competition, she won first prize for the same speech she had given in Waco.

She returned to Houston, where the *Houston Informer* reported on her success: "Miss Barbara Charline Jordan, daughter of the Reverend and Mrs. B. M. Jordan of 4910 Campbell Street . . . First place winner at the national convention contest, for which she received a $200 scholarship to the school of her choice and a medal." The article also reported that she had been chosen Girl of the Year at Wheatley by the Zeta Phi Beta sorority and that she held three district and two state championship medals in oratory. Then it quoted "Miss Jordan's response": "It's just another milestone I have passed; it's just the beginning."[29] Cocky in the face of success, Barbara Jordan showed that she believed what her Grandfather Patten had been telling her: She was special. She was riding high. She was determined to do something.

As she succeeded at debate, she grew confident, and with confidence came the ability to consider a wider range of career possibilities. Ben Jordan had always said that teaching music was the only profession open to black women at the time. But that hadn't interested Barbara. And now she was Girl of the Year as well as a national debate champion. She began to consider other opportunities more seriously. In her senior year, a visitor to Wheatley helped her make up her mind. During a Career Day program, Edith Spurlock Sampson, a black lawyer in Chicago, urged the students to consider the law. Sampson was a dynamic speaker in her own right, with an impressive résumé. An assistant state's attorney in Cook County, Illinois, she was the first woman to receive a law degree from Loyola University in Chicago. President Harry Truman had appointed her an alternate delegate to the United Nations. Until Sampson's visit, Barbara had joked with friends that they might all become lawyers; after that visit, she and fellow debate team member Otis King committed themselves to it.[30]

Ambition and direction sneaked up on Barbara Jordan. Having set her sights on Girl of the Year, she found herself enormously successful at debating. The confidence that debating brought, the recognition she received, the trip to Chicago—all combined to make her think more widely about what her future could be. She was still focused on herself, but what that self could be was now considerably enlarged. In 1952 she graduated from Wheatley and became an undergraduate at Texas Southern University, intent on entering its new law school when she was done.

6 *To Boston and Back*

Barbara Jordan began Texas Southern University with a distinct plan: She would be an undergraduate for three years and then enter its law school. It was a plan born out of her high school experience, and as she started college, there was little about it that made her think she should change the plan.[1] In many ways, college seemed to be a continuation of what was already familiar to her. Bennie was there and so were many of her friends. Although there were some new and different faces at Texas Southern, it, too, was a black school, and Jordan was still spending her time in the black wards of Houston. Both she and her sister Bennie lived with her parents, who paid their way through college. In all these ways, she was leading a life similar to her high school years. It appeared as if that would be the case right up to the moment she became a lawyer.

Jordan wanted to have a good time at Texas Southern, so she joined the Delta Sigma Theta sorority, to which Bennie belonged. To pay her dues, she babysat and cleaned houses. Even if there was much that was familiar about college, she felt more mature. The work, sorority life, and the excitement of a new place made Barbara Jordan feel that she had become an adult. Meanwhile, her father still tried to dictate her actions, which led them to fight constantly. Barbara simply refused to recognize his authority in her life, even if he was paying the bills. On one memorable occasion, the issue between them was drinking. Like many of her sorority sisters, Bennie and Barbara began to hang out at the Groovy Grill, drinking beer. Alcohol was new to Barbara's life, a part of her socializing with friends, but it was no dangerous habit for her. It didn't take long, however, before a member of Greater Pleasant Hill Baptist Church reported to Ben Jordan that the good Reverend's daughters were drinking alcohol.[2]

That evening, Ben Jordan confronted his daughters. Bennie was the first to arrive, so she received the full force of his anger. Shaken, Bennie tried weakly to justify herself. When Barbara arrived home shortly after her sister, she saw that her father was incensed, but she wasn't about to defend her actions. "What's the problem?" she asked her father curtly as he stood before her sister. "I'll tell you what the problem is," her father raged. "I have been informed that all you and your sister do at Texas Southern University is sit around and drink beer."

"Well, if somebody said that's all we do, they lied," Barbara answered. She turned on her heels, entered her room, and slammed the door.[3] Unlike Bennie, Jordan felt no need to respond further because she was a college student now. She had proven her ability to take care of her life, and she would do what she pleased, no matter what anyone reported to her father.

Jordan wanted to win awards and to receive recognition as she had in high school. During her first week of school, she decided she would run for student body president. But the dean of women told her that freshmen were not eligible to become president, so she ran for freshman president. She lost by a landslide. Undaunted, she turned to debate, where she had confidence, experience, and, it turned out, good fortune.

At Texas Southern, the debate team was coached by Tom Freeman. Part scholar and part showman, Freeman had been a student at Andover Newton Seminary in Boston, and he had received a doctorate in homiletics (preaching) from the University of Chicago. A dynamic, energizing coach, Freeman believed his duty went beyond training the students to be excellent at debate. He wanted to hone their ability to think, and he wanted to expose his students to the world beyond the segregated confines of the black wards of Houston. There were other possibilities out there; he had seen them in Boston and Chicago, and he devoted himself to ensuring his students knew of them.

Young and dedicated, Freeman was a one-man publicist and coach for his debate team. He set up contests with black and white schools throughout the Midwest and Northeast, so that his students had countless opportunities to see that wider world and to practice their debate skills. Piling his team into his new car, he drove them across the country on their debate trips.

For his sixteen-year-old prodigy, fresh from her trip to the national Ushers oratorial contest in Chicago, nothing could have been better. Tom Freeman had heard Barbara Jordan speak when she was in high school. Once he had been a judge at an Elks Oratorical Contest where Jordan was the runner-up. Freeman had

Barbara (left) and Tom Freeman (right) in a photograph of the Texas Southern University debate team

voted for her to win. He clearly saw her potential. Yet Freeman was more than a fan of Barbara Jordan; he was a teacher and a mentor. Sizing her up, he believed that she was good at presenting herself, but she needed to learn how to think and to dramatize her ideas better. Over the course of two years, Freeman nurtured her talent until she and her Wheatley classmate Otis King were his stars. The Texas Southern debate team became so well-regarded that the Harvard team traveled to compete with them during Barbara's last year at TSU. Their match ended in a tie.

At the beginning, Jordan responded both to the competition and to the excitement of traveling with the debate team. She was the first woman on his team, the first to be allowed to tour the country in a carful of males without a chaperone. Eager to appear more proper in such a group, she cut her hair, abandoned the scoop-necked dresses and jewelry, and wore less form-fitting jackets. The competitions were constantly energizing for her, but the glamour of travel faded as Jordan received an education in race relations. For the first time, she traveled through the white South, where cafes, motels, and even rest rooms in gas stations were segregated. She learned how to avoid unpleasantries, inconvenience, and hostility toward African Americans. The team packed the car with food so they didn't have to search for those few cafes in which blacks were welcome to eat. On a road map of the United States, they marked the black motels along the highways.

Yet it was impossible to pack enough food for the whole trip and impossible, without great inconvenience, to find black cafes every time they were hungry. Most of all, it was impossible not to see and feel the humiliation. That was especially true for Tom Freeman, who had lived a more dignified, respected life in the North. Barbara watched him grow incensed, especially at the gas stations, where rest rooms were reserved for "Men" and "Women" while "Colored" folk were required to use an outhouse. Tom Freeman regularly feuded with the station attendants. Once, when they were out of food, he demanded service at an all-white barbecue. They were allowed to enter by the back door and eat in the kitchen. For Jordan, traveling through the South made her realize how protected her life had been and how much a relief it was when the team would reach New York, Boston, or Chicago, where they could enter most restaurants and stay in most hotels.[8]

On May 17, 1954, two years into Jordan's college experience, the United States Supreme Court made a decision that vindicated Tom Freeman and set in motion enormous changes in American society. Thurgood Marshall and the NAACP had filed a suit on behalf of a black schoolchild in Topeka, Kansas. In *Brown* v. *The Board of Education of Topeka, Kansas*, the Supreme Court overturned *Plessy* v. *Ferguson* and ruled that segregation was unconstitutional in public schools. "Separate educational facilities are inherently unequal," the Court declared in its decision. Segregated schools inhibit "the educational and mental development of Negro children," the Court explained:

> To separate them from others of similar age and qualifications solely because of their race generates a feeling of inferiority as to their status in the community that may affect their hearts and minds in a way unlikely ever to be undone.[9]

Across the country, African American communities celebrated the landmark decision. Barbara Jordan responded, "So finally." She regretted that the decision had not come earlier, so that her high school and elementary school could have been integrated. Yet Jordan was glad that she, a college student, would be a witness to history, the schools of Houston integrating before her very eyes.[10]

Segregation did not suddenly end, however. Fiercely opposed to integration, the city of Houston and the state of Texas did more than dig in their heels. Texas was defiant. In 1956, led by Democratic Governor Allan Shivers, the state government passed laws that guaranteed school segregation, outlawed intermarriage between African Americans and white Americans, prohibited the burial of blacks and whites in the same cemetery, and required all who believed in integration to register themselves with the state. Texas asserted it could do so because a state had the right to overrule unwarranted federal interference in its affairs.[11] It would take more than twelve years before the first signs of integration appeared in the Houston public schools.

In other parts of the South, African Americans led organized acts of civil disobedience to integrate public life. In Montgomery, Alabama, on December 1, 1955, Rosa Parks refused to stand up and move to the back of a segregated city bus to accommodate a white passenger. Empowered to enforce the segregation laws, the bus driver promptly arrested her. A modest, almost selfless woman, Ms. Parks was a seamstress at a Montgomery department store but also the secretary of the local chapter of the NAACP. Her jailing sparked the Montgomery Bus Boycott, which lasted for more than a year, until late December 1956. During it, local African Americans organized into private car pools to avoid riding the buses. In spite of arrests, threats, and the bombings of black churches and homes, Montgomery African Americans brought the city bus company to near bankruptcy. The organizing force behind that boycott was the Montgomery Improvement Association, a black civic group composed of ministers and other African Americans in Montgomery. Its president was the Reverend Dr. Martin Luther King Jr. In the end, the United States Supreme Court confirmed that the segregation of Montgomery buses was unconstitutional. The Montgomery bus boycott drew the attention of the country, raising new concerns about the injustice of segregation and new hopes among African Americans that segregation could be dismantled.[12]

News of such experience changed Barbara Jordan. The resistance of Houston and Texas to integration sobered her; the *Brown* v. *Board of Education* Supreme Court decision inspired her. At the Southern Forensic Conference, an integrated debate at Baylor University in Waco, Texas, she won first prize. But her victory felt somehow hollow to her.[13] In high school, she had expected that segregation would not end during her lifetime; better, she had thought, to be special and different among black people and get on with her life. Now, however, she saw that the weight of the law was against segregation, and it made her feel that her personal ambitions should be dedicated toward helping integration succeed. What good would another medal do for that? she asked herself. She had found the white people at the Waco contest "no competition at all."[14] So why couldn't she be a success among white people and use her success to force integration? she thought. She wanted to do her part to speed change. Years later, she remembered that moment:

> I woke to the necessity that someone had to push integration along in a private way if it were ever going to come. That was on my mind continually at that period—that some black people could make it in this white man's world, and that those who could had to do it. They had to move.[15]

Jordan was still focused upon making a success of herself. But for the first time, she had dedicated herself to a public goal, which set in motion a number of changes in her life. She no longer felt it would be enough to go to law school at Texas Southern; she needed to think about succeeding at a law school in the white world. She remembered her first meeting with the advisors to the pre-law program at Texas Southern, when she had entered school. When she had asked what particular courses she needed to take, they had told her it didn't matter; she just needed credits.[16] Her advisors' comments now struck her as odd. As a new student, Jordan couldn't have known that the university lacked a well-organized curriculum. In fact, Texas Southern was a new school, hastily fashioned out of older schools for blacks in 1947, so that the state of Texas might claim that there was a separate and presumably "equal" education provided African Americans in the state. The resources of Texas Southern were divided between vocational training in such fields as cleaning and pressing, auto mechanics, and shoe repair on the one hand, and liberal arts training in such disciplines as English, physics, and chemistry on the other.[17] She may not have understood that the university was still developing its program, but Jordan sensed that her prelaw advisers hadn't given her adequate advice. She was sure she needed a more focused undergraduate program. So she decided to stay at Texas Southern for four years, earn a bachelor's degree in political science, and then apply to law schools.

Jordan had no idea what law schools might be available to her, but she allowed herself to dream big. After Barbara and Otis King debated Harvard to a tie, she announced to Tom Freeman that she wanted to go to Harvard Law School. "You can't get in," he told her. The undergraduate debate team at Harvard might have heard of them, he added, but "they have never heard of Texas Southern University at Harvard Law School."[18]

Boston University Law School, Freeman advised, was a possibility.

At home, she announced to her father that she wanted to go to Boston University for law school and asked him to pay her way. Ben Jordan read through the costs of tuition, room, board, and books. "This is more money than I have ever spent on anything or anyone," he said. "But if you want to go," he added, "we'll manage."[19] For Ben Jordan and the rest of the Jordans, it was a moment of great dedication to Barbara. While Ben Jordan covered tuition, room, and board, Rose Mary and Bennie, now music teachers, agreed to pay for Barbara's books and spending money. For her part, Barbara would have to remain in Boston for the entire school year because there would be no money for visits during the holidays. That didn't matter to Jordan. It didn't even matter what Boston or the law school was like. She was certain of her goal. In the fall of 1956, she entered law school at Boston University.[20]

In Boston, Barbara Jordan lived among white people for the first time. By coincidence, there were two African American women from Houston in the entering law school class, Jordan and Issie Shelton, former Girl of the Year at Jack Yates High School.[21]

Even though Barbara had traveled to northern cities and competed against white debaters, she had yet to live in what she called the "white man's world." White people in this integrated community, she soon learned, were not as receptive to blacks as they might first appear. Growing up in Houston, she knew that the color line—the distinction between the experience of being black and being white—was written into the daily lives of everyone. It made a difference in where one lived, where one went to school, and whom one loved. It affected where one worked, what one worked at, and what one earned. Hidden from and even forbidden to her in Texas, the experience of whites appeared curious and strange to Barbara Jordan.

Yet at Boston University Law School, she found that a color line existed as well, in a city where integration was legal. She felt no hostility, but there were limits to how friendly and how open white students were to her. They accepted her but did not socialize with her beyond going out for an occasional cup of coffee. No black was invited into any of the white study groups that law students organized. In the dormitory on Rawley Street where Jordan lived, there was one other law student, Louise Bailey, daughter of the Democratic National Committee chairman in 1956. Louise Bailey was more than an acquaintance. She once borrowed money from Barbara. But at Christmas time, Jordan somehow knew that she would not get an invitation to visit Bailey's home in Hartford, Connecticut, as much as Jordan wished it otherwise. Bailey simply called Jordan in the dormitories to wish her happy holidays. From such experiences, Jordan began to suspect that Boston would be lonely and isolating for her.[22]

As it turned out, she was too busy studying to worry about such matters. She found law school difficult and disorienting. For the first time in her education, she was being asked to provide not only the answer to a question but also the reasons for the solutions she came to. She was being judged on how she arrived at an answer and how many approaches to an answer she understood. The focus was on logic, reasoning, and justifications. It was so new and strange that it scared her. The other students had come from good schools and often had experience in law offices. They had an advantage over her, she felt. In her law classes, the professors used a technical language, with words such as "lessors," "lessees," "litigants," "plaintiffs," "promisors," and "promissees." It made her feel all the more disoriented. She had begun the school year believing, as she always did, that she would quickly become one of the top students and write for the student *Law Review*. By the end of the first semester, she was convinced that she had flunked at least one of her exams.

But she did not flunk. She simply lost the illusion that she would be able to make *Law Review*. For the first time, she realized that in spite of her intelligence she would have to study hard and long to make up for the difference between her and the other students at the school, most of whom were much better prepared. She was embarrassed that she did not understand the material, so she began to study in the dormitory or in her room rather than the law library. She rarely slept more than three or four hours a night. In the spring, she realized that it was impossible to learn the concepts or absorb all the information without talking about it. So she joined the black study group.[23]

She gained enough confidence that she enjoyed when the professors called on her in class. But that did not happen often. Boston University Law School was a man's world. Among Jordan's entering class of 250, only 6 students were women. And professors did not take the women students as seriously, calling on them in class only on designated "Ladies Days."[24]

For all her hard work, her improvement seemed only modest. Jordan began to suspect that her education at Texas Southern and at Phillis Wheatley had been poor. She had thought that her success at debate and oratory signified the success of her education. But now she thought of that as what she called "speechifying." The ideas were always written out on note cards beforehand and then presented; the emphasis was on how well you could make that presentation. Speechifying was beautiful and important, but there was a difference, she now believed, between presenting an idea and reasoning, proving, or defending it. No one taught her that in grade school or high school. No one had challenged her to do that at Texas Southern. For the first time, she felt she was being genuinely educated.

Yet it made her think of segregation once more. She decided Texas Southern was an "instant university," thrown together to fight off integration. She felt that an education in segregated schools placed her and all black college students at a disadvantage. "The best training available in an all-black instant university was not equal to the best training one developed as a white university student," she thought. As a result, at Boston University Law School, she had to catch up. She "was doing sixteen years of remedial work in thinking." Jordan buckled down still harder. She rarely went out. At the end of the school year, she flew home, uncertain if she had passed.

She did pass, however, and by the second year, she had improved enough to be noticed by at least one professor, who told her she had potential. Slowly, law school became easier, enough so that she could enjoy an occasional party at the apartment of Bill Gibson, a fellow member of her study group.

Meanwhile, in Little Rock, Arkansas, in September of 1957, the federal government took the first step toward ensuring that the South would integrate its schools. President Dwight Eisenhower reluctantly forced Arkansas Governor Orval Faubus to admit black students to all-white Central High School. On television, the nation watched as an angry mob of white parents and ardent segregationists attacked black students and black reporters. Days later, it watched again as Eisenhower ordered riot-trained troops from the 101st Airborne Division of the Army to secure Little Rock and protect black citizens.

An angry Arkansas crowd harasses
Elizabeth Eckford on September 4, 1957.

As she struggled with the difficulties of school and the tension over segregation in the South, Barbara Jordan found comfort from a surprising source, the minister of the Boston University Chapel. He was Howard Thurman, the first African American to be head of the University Chapel and one of the most renowned black ministers in the United States. Devoted to integration, Thurman preached a radically different faith from what Barbara Jordan grew up with. From her father, she had learned that religion told you what you shouldn't do; from Thurman, a minister who had blended many different faiths into his belief, the focus was on learning to live now and to treat other people well.[28] It made Jordan think that her goal to help along integration was religious because it was part of an effort to treat people well.

Jordan's third and final year of law school was her best as a student in spite of a tragedy. Grandfather Patten died. In the last years of his life, his beloved granddaughter away at law school, John Edward Patten had begun to drink excessively. Drunk one day, he stumbled onto the railroad tracks and was run over by a train. Grandfather Patten was barely alive, his legs lost at the hip. On his death bed at the hospital, he pleaded that Barbara not see him like this, but she was already on her way. He died holding her hand.[29]

Grieving, Jordan returned to Boston and finished the school year. Her parents, Rose Mary, and Bennie insisted they drive up from Houston for her graduation ceremony. There, to their delight, they watched Barbara cross the graduation stage and receive her diploma, a scroll of paper tied with a red ribbon. It had been a grueling experience for many of the law students. The graduating class had shrunk from its original 250 to 128 students.[30] Of them, Issie Shelton and Barbara Jordan were the only two women. Alone in her dormitory room, the stress of those three, difficult years finally over, Barbara Jordan burst into tears.[31]

Jordan stayed in Boston for the summer of 1959 to prepare for and to take the Massachusetts Bar exam. For a short time, she considered remaining in Boston because it was freer of segregation than Texas. She applied for a job as a claims-processing lawyer at the John Hancock Insurance Company. But she felt no roots in Boston. Instead, she felt anonymous and isolated. She had lived among white people for three years, long enough to understand better how to meet, to socialize, and perhaps to work with them. But she had no allies, no family, and no resources to help her along in Boston. At the end of the summer, she returned to Houston.[32]

1 A Politician Is Born

With the exception of studying for the Texas bar exam, the twenty-three-year-old Jordan had no idea what she would do next. She passed the exam. She also received notice that she had passed the Massachusetts Bar exam, but she had no desire to return to Boston. She lived with her parents on Campbell Street and used their dining room as a makeshift office, from which she represented a few people in divorce cases and wrote petitions and wills for the occasional other client. Her father bought her a small car so that she could travel back and forth between the courthouse and Campbell Street. At best, she was making only a small attempt to practice law. Outside of her modest work life, she still loved a good time. For two years, between 1959 and 1961, Barbara and Bennie fell into a routine of late-night music and drinks at a local bar. They continued their nights on the town until Bennie married.

By then, however, Jordan had begun to think about politics for the first time. After living in the North,

Jordan saw Houston through new eyes. In the 1950s and 1960s, the economy of the city was booming as oil, chemicals, and gas became ever more valuable commodities. From the refining and transporting of oil, the manufacturing of chemical products, and the piping of natural gas, a new generation of wealth developed in Houston. In turn, it developed the city. Everywhere one looked in downtown Houston, the signs of growth were apparent. The very skyline of the city changed. For the first time, skyscrapers rose in the business center, and the Houston Astrodome, the first indoor sports stadium in the country, was built.[1]

Yet African Americans had not succeeded as other citizens of Houston had. They remained virtually segregated from the growing Houston business community. They were poor compared with most of the white citizens of the city. Their neighborhoods had the worst city services and bore the brunt of the pollution from the newly built oil refineries. They had only begun to gain admittance to public schools that had been for whites only. Throughout the late 1960s, protests continued over the quality of education available in the black wards.

The income of African Americans was hardly better than in the decades before. Between 50 and 60 percent of all African Americans in Houston earned less than $4,000 per year. The federal definition of poverty in 1959 was an annual income below $3,000. Yet one quarter of African Americans earned less than $2,000.[2] Most blacks were not business proprietors; they worked for other people. African Americans owned only 3 percent of the businesses in Houston, yet they made up between 20 and 25 percent of the population of the city. They still had not gained access to many jobs on the public payroll that were vital to the community. Less than four percent of the police force was black.[3]

These conditions inspired Jordan to seek change through political participation. First, however, she decided to set up a law office. For that, she needed a little money. To finance her office space, she taught a course in government at the Tuskegee Institute in Alabama during the summer of 1961. Ben Jordan was dismayed. Tuskegee had lost some of its appeal for him, and he had greater expectations of his daughter now that she was a lawyer. Barbara reassured him that she had a plan.

In the fall of 1961, she opened her law office, renting rooms in a building on Lyons Avenue in the Fifth Ward with another new lawyer, Asbury Butler. She was in the heart of the business district of the Fifth Ward, in the middle of the neighborhood she had known all her life. Across the street was the grocery store owned by Charles White Sr., father of her Wheatley high school friend.[4]

Practicing law never became the center of Jordan's life. She thought that her office was valuable because it made her more visible in her community, and with visibility, she would be able to run for political office. In the months before she set up her practice, politics had become a new passion for Jordan. Two things had caused her to have a new sense of direction in her life: The political landscape of the country and of Houston had recently changed; and she had become active in the Democratic party.

In the two years since she had returned to Houston, the civil-rights movement had entered a new phase. After the Montgomery bus boycott, there was a relative lull in organized protests against segregation. Then, in February 1960, four black college students sat down at the whites-only lunch counter of a Woolworth's in downtown Greensboro, North Carolina. They were refused service but sat there peacefully all day. Their protest was a spontaneous action, but within days, it became an organized event among black college students in the area. Five days later, 400 students were participating, and the protest spread to another segregated lunch counter nearby. Within one week, sit-in protests spread to many cities in North Carolina. It was not long before the movement spread across the South.[5]

On March 4, 1960, Texas Southern University students began a sit-in protest at the segregated lunch counter of Weingarten's Department Store in downtown Houston. Soon they organized themselves into the Progressive Youth Association. Their actions continued, with some interruptions, for the next six months, the protests quickly spreading to nearby Henke and Pillot supermarkets, and from there to the lunch counters at Walgreen's, Mading's, and Woolworth's. Eventually, students targeted the segregated cafeteria at City Hall. A few restaurants and cafeterias served the students, but the most common response of store owners was to close their lunch counters.

Students became a potent, political force in other southern cities, but in Houston their protests were less successful. Fewer than a hundred students participated. While the city formed a negotiating committee between white business owners and black community leaders, it failed to reach any agreement to integrate. Still more troubling, several African Americans were attacked by whites who were outraged by the protest.

*The first Woolworth's sit-in, February 2, 1960.
Left to right: Joseph McNeill, Frar McCain, Billy
Smith, and Clarence Henderson*

The white newspapers were unsympathetic, as were some black establishment leaders. The city of Houston was not about to allow protesters to rule the day.

Jordan was uncomfortable with the protest, but she sensed that the mood of the country was changing. With the right people in politics, she thought, something might be done about segregation and other injustices in American society. Jordan's idea of politics, however, was different from that of the protesters. By politics, she meant the process by which people are elected to public office or work with the city, state, and federal government to change the laws. Jordan was inspired by the same ideals as the student activists, and she felt anger about racial discrimination. She once said that the history of slavery, violence, and prejudice against African Americans made all blacks "militant in their guts." She passionately believed in equality and fought against segregation.

But with one exception in 1965, Jordan did not participate in protests. Even if Dr. Martin Luther King Jr. and other civil-rights activists used them successfully, she considered protests and civil disobedience to be acts of confrontation. She thought that they made the protesters appear to be rabble-rousers rather than respectable members of the community. It was a sign that Jordan, now an adult, had been influenced by Ben Jordan. Raised in a conservative home with a dominating father, Jordan had come to believe that confrontation with the more powerful did not work. To be truly effective in politics, she declared, one must "work her way through the system. . . . Disruptive or divisive behavior is of no help."

She was nonetheless dedicated to civil rights, and she saw that the country was changing. Even in

Houston, which resisted mightily, change slowly occurred. Organizing among black voters had led to the election of Mrs. Charles White, an African American and former schoolteacher, to the school board in 1958.[9] In the summer of 1960, Barbara entered politics for the first time. She volunteered for the campaign of the Democratic candidates for president and vice president of the United States: Senator John F. Kennedy of Massachusetts and Senator Lyndon B. Johnson of Texas. She passionately believed Kennedy and Johnson stood for justice and equality for all Americans.[10]

Jordan didn't yet imagine that she would be elected to office. But that soon changed. In the late summer and fall, she helped the Democrats develop a block-worker program for the black precincts in Harris County, in which Houston is located. The block-worker program was directed by Chris Dixie, a labor lawyer and liberal Democrat who was an influential person among Harris County Democrats. Its other members were John Butler and Versie Shelton. The program was designed to get out the vote, which was traditionally Democratic in the black precincts. The block workers were neighborhood recruits who volunteered to get voters to the polls on election day.

To recruit block workers, the four campaign workers traveled to churches, schools, and clubs in the precincts, where Versie Shelton gave a presentation. One night, when Versie Shelton was sick, Jordan spoke in her place. At a black church in the Fifth Ward, Jordan's talk stirred the audience into action unlike any recruiting speech before.[11] From that moment on, Jordan became a regular speaker for the effort to get out the Democratic vote. She spoke not only to black organizations but also to liberal, white Democratic groups that believed in integration. She became particularly popular with the Steelworker's Union locals, but she also won over several other labor unions. In the election in November, 80 percent of all black voters in Harris County went to the polls, the highest African American turnout for any city in the South.[12]

*J*ordan had found a new calling with an old, familiar appeal. Speaking before those enthusiastic groups, Jordan was reminded of all of her successes debating at Wheatley and Texas Southern. It was still exciting to be in the limelight. Even better, the rewards for her speeches were the advancement of political causes she believed in and the election of people to power. She had been bored with law and lonely because Bennie was now married. But this campaign filled her time and inspired her.

After the Kennedy-Johnson campaign ended in victory in November 1960, Jordan became increasingly active in local politics. First, she joined the Harris County Democrats, one of two Democratic factions in the county. The conservative faction excluded minorities as well as labor representatives. But the Harris County Democrats were controlled by white liberals. They appeared receptive to Barbara and sympathetic to the large African American constituency in the county. Jordan also became a member of the NAACP and the Harris County Council of Organizations (HCCO), the most politically active black organization in Harris County. Soon she was an officer of HCCO and the president of the Houston Lawyers Association, a black legal organization. She spoke regularly on behalf of the Harris County Democrats, especially at the beginning of 1962, when they organized a voter registration drive.[13]

Jordan's increased participation in politics made her more visible to the political establishment. She was now a good candidate for public office. Early that same year, Chris Dixie proposed that she run on the Harris County Democratic slate for the Texas House of Representatives. She would be one of twelve candidates on the slate, the rest of them white. Because nearly all people in the county voted Democratic, the real challenge to winning was the upcoming Democratic primary. She would be paired off in the primary against Willis Whatley, a conservative. Jordan hesitated only because she didn't have the $500 filing fee to become a candidate. But Dixie pulled out five $100 bills and loaned her the money on the spot.[14]

For Jordan, the campaign was a kind of baptism in Texas politics. It began in an encouraging fashion. Reverend Albert Lucas of Good Hope and the other ministers in the black wards of Houston raised the money to cover Jordan's filing fee. Through her Aunt Mamie and Mamie's husband, Wilmer Lee, she received the endorsement of Hobart Taylor, the wealthiest African American in Houston. Mack Hannah, an influential black banker, supported her, as did the HCCO and the Harris County AFL-CIO, the dominant coalition of labor unions.[15]

Her speeches on the campaign trail made her optimistic. Jordan and the other candidates were running for at-large positions. An at-large position meant that each of them represented the entire county and had to be elected by all the voters of the county; no one could be elected to represent a specific community only, such as the Fifth Ward. Jordan and the other eleven candidates made joint appearances throughout Harris County. From her first speech before a white liberal group, when the audience gave her a standing ovation, she was well received. She mixed her message of principles and ideals of equality and civil rights with practical information on what she would do if she were elected to office. She researched the legislature carefully, so that she spoke intelligently about the reforms she wanted, from state budgeting procedures to the distribution of state money to black and white colleges. She campaigned hard in both the black and the white liberal areas of Harris County. Chris Dixie estimated that she would win 90 percent of the black vote and 30 per cent of the white vote. "There's no way you can lose," he said.[16]

But she lost. She got 46,000 votes to Willis Whatley's 65,000 votes.[17] Stunned, she tried to understand why. All the other candidates on the Harris County slate, who were white, had won. She had been well supported in the black community. White liberals had endorsed her and cheered her, but most whites had voted for Whatley. Chris Dixie told her not to be discouraged. It was only her first campaign.

She was determined to try again in two years, but she needed a better explanation for her loss. Once, during the election, a professor and political pollster at Rice University had told her there were three reasons it would be difficult for her to win: she was black, she was a woman, and she was large.[18] After her loss, she began to believe there was some truth in what he had said. In the complicated politics of Houston, conservative Democrats were powerful and well financed. They were the political establishment of Houston, and they excluded blacks from their inner circle. The *Houston*

Chronicle and the *Houston Post*, the major daily newspapers of the city, had endorsed Whatley. Racial discrimination was even more of a problem for Jordan's election in the largely white areas of Harris County outside of Houston. Virtually no one voted for Jordan there. As she campaigned, Jordan had thought that "the black and woman stuff were just side issues" that people would ignore.[19] After the election, she decided that she had been naive.

Between 1962 and 1964, the civil rights movement continued to push for integration in the South. Civil-rights activists also began to organize voter registration campaigns among black voters. At moments, the attention of the nation was fixed on the South, where students, ministers, and activists continued to oppose segregation through sit-ins at segregated businesses and restaurants. News clips on television carried the accounts of antisegregation efforts in Birmingham, Alabama. There, police chief Eugene "Bull" Connor led the attack on civil-rights activists. Bull Connor unleashed police dogs on civil-rights protesters and sprayed the activists with high-pressure fire hoses. The images on television horrified many people.

In response, more Americans—black and white—became sympathetic to the civil-rights movement. During the summer of 1963, black leaders organized the March on Washington in support of civil rights. More than 250,000 people from across the country gathered on the Mall before the Washington Monument. It was a historic event. There, Martin Luther King Jr. gave his "I Have a Dream" speech. The March on Washington was the first mass meeting of its kind to be covered by television and radio. The nation appeared to be recognizing the plight of African Americans.[20]

From this greater attention to civil rights, Jordan gained faith that more whites would support African Americans in their struggle for justice and in politics. In 1964 she ran again to be an at-large representative to

The Birmingham Fire Department turns a hose on civil-rights demonstrators, July 15, 1963.

Dr. Martin Luther King Jr. delivering his speech,
"I Have a Dream," August 28, 1963

the Texas State Legislature from Harris County. She lost
again. Since 1962 she had increased her activity in the
community. She had worked on behalf of the NAACP
to integrate schools in Houston and to increase job

opportunities for African Americans. But it had not mattered. Frustrated and discouraged, she couldn't bring herself to go to campaign headquarters the night of the election.[21] It simply did not matter how much support she had in the black community. As long as the at-large system was in place, she believed, "black voters could help white liberals get elected, but could not represent themselves."[22]

The second loss brought her to a crisis. She began to wonder whether or not she should continue in politics. She was black and female; it seemed to make all the difference. Meanwhile her parents and her friends were pressuring her to get married. Rose Mary and Bennie were married. If she wasn't going to be successful in politics, they said, then she should at least have a family.

At some point during that time, Jordan made a decision. She preferred to spend her life in the public eye rather than marry. She chose to remain in politics. She didn't believe that she could both raise a family and be a politician. She didn't want to do both.

But she also knew that she would be going against public expectations in 1964. At the time, most people thought that all women should want a family. Jordan believed that the public had a different standard for women than for men. If a woman wanted to pursue a career, it would have to be in addition to a family. The attitude irritated Jordan because she knew it would be different for a man: "No one said to him that he needed to care for the babies, or iron the curtains, or clean the johns. What was expected was that he'd marry a woman to do it."[23]

She made a decision that she would have to change public perception. She would have "to bring the public along to understand that there are some women for whom other expectations are possible."[24] It was that simple and that difficult. As her Grandfather Patten had hoped, she was going to be her own person. But as he also predicted, it would be hard to do. She told her family and friends that she would make a decision about her marrying "down the road a piece."[25] It was her way of avoiding the controversy as she developed her political career.

Jordan vowed she would not be a three-time loser. Instead, she would be patient, work hard, and slowly build a reputation and a following. Only months before, she had been discouraged. Now she was dedicated to her success. She helped her cause when she got a full-time job as the administrative assistant to County Judge Bill Elliott. Elliot was a liberal and a highly influential member of the Houston political establishment. As a county judge, Elliott was as much an administrator as a judge. Barbara's appointment made her his representative to welfare agencies, Community Council projects, and other organizations to which the county contributed. It was the first time an African American had held such a position. The major daily newspapers in Houston printed photos of her and carried news stories reporting her appointment. Her work gave her valuable contacts throughout the county.[26]

Meanwhile, to save additional money, Jordan practiced law in the evenings. She also participated in a protest for the first and only time. In spite of numerous court orders and petitions, the Houston public school system remained almost entirely segregated. Jordan had worked actively for the NAACP to integrate the schools, but the city of Houston had virtually ignored orders to desegregate. By 1965, however, even she had reached her limit. She helped to organize a student boycott of the Houston schools that was led by the Reverend Bill Lawson and several members of the local NAACP. State money is given to schools based on the size of daily attendance. The boycott cost the school district dearly when thousands of students were absent. The day of the boycott, about three thousand of the protesters marched quietly to city hall. The event pressured school board members to accelerate desegregation, which was completed in 1966. Jordan's role increased her reputation in the black community and added to her political base.[27]

At the same time, Jordan waited patiently for the right political office to become available. Even if 250,000 people rallied for civil rights on the Washington Mall, it was clear to Jordan that most Texans were against racial equality. They would resist at every turn any laws or government actions to bring it about. Help would have to come from someplace outside of Texas.

It came from a Texan in the White House and from the United States Supreme Court. In July 1964, under strong pressure from President Lyndon Johnson, the former senator from Texas, the United States Congress passed into law a Civil Rights Act. The law guaranteed all people equal rights in employment and equal access to all public places in the United States. No employer could refuse someone a job, fire a person, or otherwise discriminate against him on the basis of "race, color, sex, religion, or national origin."[28]

In addition, all individuals regardless of "race or color" were entitled to "full and equal enjoyment" of "places of public accommodation." That meant hotels, motels, buses, trains, planes, ships, theaters, restaurants, and any other public places had to be integrated.[29] For the first time, federal laws guaranteed all citizens this right. The government had long since guaranteed the right to federal employees. Now the South and any other region of the country would have to integrate its public accommodations.

Reaction in Texas to the new law was strong, swift, and discouraging for Jordan. Only four of the twenty-four Texans in the House of Representatives and Senate voted for the Civil Rights Act of 1964. Democratic Governor John Connally of Texas publicly declared his opposition to the public accommodations portion of the act. Months later, at the Democratic state convention in Texas, Connally torpedoed Jordan's nomination to the executive committee of the party. He said that the party was not yet ready for an African American in such a position.[30]

Jordan began to dislike Connally intensely. Then, a series of Supreme Court decisions helped her to put Connally out of her mind by making Connally's resistance to equality less important and Jordan's opportunity to win public office possible. Beginning with *Baker* v. *Carr* in 1962, the Supreme Court began to assert its right to review whether or not legislative districts within states violated the Constitution. Then, in a 1963 decision, Justice William O. Douglas declared that legislative districts must be shaped or allocated so that they give blacks and women voting power equal to that of all other people. The Equal Protection clause of the Fourteenth Amendment guarantees it, the Court said. Finally, in 1964, the ruling of the Court in four cases made it clear: Whatever legislative districts are drawn up, they must not "debase or dilute" the voting strength of blacks because that would be a form of discrimination. Legislative districts must reflect the equal voting power of African Americans.

One of those cases, *Kilgarlin* v. *Martin*, required the Texas legislature to abolish at-large legislative districts in urban areas. In their place, the legislature would have to create smaller, distinctly individualized districts. If the population of Harris County entitled it to twelve representatives in the state legislature, they would have to represent twelve separate parts of the city and county.[31]

Within a year, in spite of strong resistance among conservatives, Harris County was forced to create individual legislative districts to replace its single "at-large" district. Barbara Jordan was suddenly in the new Eleventh State Senatorial District, which included the Fifth Ward of Houston. Thirty-eight percent of its voters were African Americans, and the remainder were mostly white labor-union members and Mexican Americans.[32] All of them would be receptive to a Jordan candidacy for state senator. Her decision to run was easy.

Jordan's 1966 campaign for the Texas Senate had a controversy, however. J. C. "Charlie" Whitfield Jr. wanted to run for the office. Whitfield was an incumbent state representative. He was also a white liberal, with strong support from the labor unions and from the Harris County Democrats. But Jordan had learned from the experience of her two losses, and she felt that she deserved the position. She was ready to fight hard for it. When Whitfield notified Jordan that he was going to run, she immediately quit her job with Bill Elliott and devoted herself full-time to campaigning.

The real competition this time was to receive the endorsement of the Harris County Democrats Executive Committee. On the ballot, the candidate of the Harris County Democrats would effectively win the election because of its influence among unions, blacks, and liberals. The members of the executive committee had always endorsed Whitfield for state representative. But they endorsed Barbara Jordan this time. Jordan was not only one of their shining lights, they decided, but black voters needed representation. She was more deserving.[33]

Charlie Whitfield was enraged. He fought the endorsement at the general meeting of the Harris County Democrats, and when he lost there, he proclaimed he would run anyway. Jordan was ready for him. She established a campaign headquarters on Lyons Avenue because it was near her office and in the heart of the Fifth Ward. She secured the endorsement of organized labor. To ensure the success of her block-worker program, she ran it herself.

As the election neared, Charlie Whitfield sent out campaign flyers across the district. In them he declared that he was the more qualified candidate. He said that the Harris County Democrats were forced to endorse Jordan because she was black. Whitfield challenged the black voters of the district not to vote as a block. Don't vote simply on the basis of race; don't create "a seat for a member of the NEGRO race," he declared. Instead, he urged, the black community should consider experience as well, which should lead them to vote for him over Barbara Jordan.[34]

As a political tactic, the flyer was a huge mistake. It incensed black voters and made Whitfield a pariah among white liberals. But Jordan would not take any chances that Charlie Whitfield might succeed. She was ready to play hardball. In speeches throughout her dis-

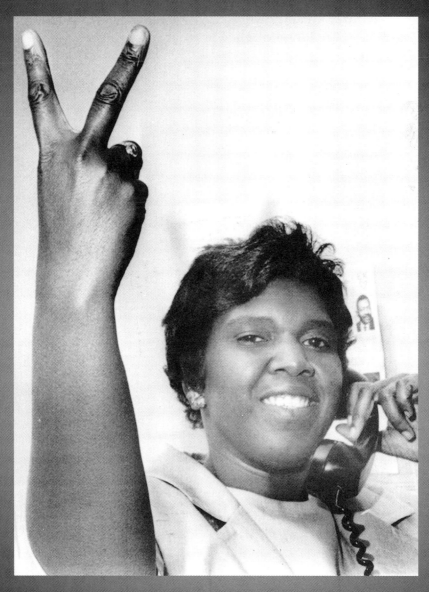

Barbara Jordan shows the "V for Victory" sign after winning the Democratic nomination to the Texas Senate, May 7, 1966.

trict, she answered Whitfield: "Look, don't tell us about black block votes. You know white folks have been block-voting for the past century. . . . Our time has come."[35] The black community had been patient for a century. Now, she told her audience, it was their turn. Her victory would be their turn.

In the Democratic primary of May 1966, Jordan received twice the number of votes as Whitfield and went on to become the first black woman in the Texas Senate and the first African American state senator in nearly a hundred years. At the same time, Curtis Graves became the first black state representative from Houston in seventy-one years. It was a small but noticeable change in Texas politics. The two of them made national news, including *The New York Times* and *Time* magazine.[36]

On primary election night, once her victory was clear, the thirty-year old Jordan drove with her family to a nearby celebration. At Lyons Avenue, windows were flung open and crowds of people lined the street. They screamed when they saw her, their new state senator. At the victory party, cameras and microphones were everywhere. Beaming, she told the reporters that she was "still kind of numb. But it feels great, just great."[37] She was black and female, but she had won the primary in spite of these supposed hurdles. She went on to victory in the fall elections of 1966.

8 Among the Good Old Boys

When the Texas State Senate convened in January 1967, its spectators' gallery was filled with hundreds of African Americans from Houston. They had driven to Austin for Barbara Jordan's first day. The gallery audience cheered as Jordan appeared on the Senate floor followed by her family. Jordan smiled, embarrassed but proud, as she looked up at the crowd of black faces.

Yet she also felt her new responsibility, and it worried her. Her supporters expected a lot from their new senator. They were proud of her accomplishment, but their excitement was born out of hopes they had for themselves as well. She had promised them that her election was their victory, too: Finally someone would speak for the interests of a community that was very much in need. Jordan's constituents wanted their streets improved and their neighborhoods protected. They wanted better schools for their children, and they wanted jobs and training for themselves, according to their abilities.

Barbara Jordan knew that getting anything done for her district would require time. First she needed to understand the politics of the Texas Senate, which meant that she needed to find allies within it. She needed also to find a way to disarm the resistance she would face to passing the laws she favored. Accomplishing that would not be easy. Jordan entered a world unlike any that she had encountered before. In the previous term of the Senate, there had been one woman, Neveille Colson. But redistricting, which gave Jordan a seat in Houston, had eliminated Colson's district 60 miles (97 kilometers) away.[2] Jordan was the only woman among more than 30 senators. The institution was literally not equipped for her. Colson had been forced to use a bathroom two floors up from the Senate chamber. With the arrival of Jordan, a new lounge and bathroom was remodeled just off the floor of the Senate. It soon came to be known as the "Barbara Jordan Memorial Bathroom."

If the senators were unaccustomed to women among them, they were even less accustomed to African Americans and less hospitable. Many of them made no bones about their feelings for the new senator from the eleventh district. Privately, Senator A.M. Aiken of Paris, Texas, a senior member of the Senate, confessed that he had never treated a black person as an equal. On the day the Senate session began, Dorsey Hardeman of San Angelo, one of the most powerful members of the Senate, told another senator that he "wasn't going to let no nigger woman tell him what to do."[3] At the very least, the other senators were nervous and hostile.

The Texas State Senate reflected the history of southern politics since the end of Reconstruction in 1877. Like most legislatures in the South, the Texas

Senate was dominated by Democrats as a matter of tradition. Most Texans did not like the Republican party. They identified it as the party of Abraham Lincoln, which had controlled the federal government during the Civil War and had tried to take away the power of the individual states during Reconstruction. The Republican-led government in Washington sent federal troops into the southern states to protect the constitutional rights of African Americans. It was during Reconstruction, under Republican leadership, that blacks last served as state representatives and state senators.

When southern whites had retaken control of southern state legislatures after 1877, they did so as Democrats. That was still the case in 1967, ninety years later. While there were liberal Democrats in the mold of President Franklin Delano Roosevelt, it was common for southern Democrats to be segregationists and still more racist. They represented the extreme, conservative wing of the Democratic party. Yet as a bloc within their political party, southern Democrats had formidable power in state and also national politics. A Confederate flag still flew above the statehouse in Austin.[4]

Jordan entered the Texas State Senate along with approximately ten liberal-leaning senators, who were happy to see her elected. Yet that left more than two-thirds of the state senators who didn't like her being there.[5] She was truly exploring new and foreign territory.

Jordan quickly developed a strategy to become an insider, a style of politics she would rely upon throughout her political career. Her first decision was to show other senators that no matter what her experience, she would keep the affairs of the Texas Senate quiet. When reporters asked her what it felt like to be a black woman among all those conservative white men in the Senate, she responded sarcastically: "As it turned out, the Capitol stayed on its foundations and the star didn't fall off the top."[6] To the other senators, Jordan's response made it clear that she was tactful. She wasn't going to complain aloud about other senators' treatment of her. Whatever resentment or frustration she might feel, she wasn't going to voice that to the press or to the public. She wanted the other senators to trust her to be a member of their club. That way, she believed, she would get along with her colleagues.

She became a good student of Senate operations. She researched each committee to determine how it was organized and which of the committees would bring her the most influence in the areas she preferred. When she met with Lieutenant Governor Preston Smith, who determined the committee assignments for each senator, she requested State Affairs and Labor and Management Relations. Smith was fully aware that she was a newsworthy figure, whose publicity could reflect upon him. He granted her those two committee assignments and nine others.

Then Jordan began to cultivate a relationship with the most powerful senators. She wanted them to feel that they didn't have to change their ways because she was around. If they were uncertain how they should speak with her and how to work with her, then she did her best to make them consider her as one of the crowd. These were men who were used to carrying on the work of the Senate in the private, whites-only clubs of Austin and on hunting trips in the surrounding areas. They had a strong sense of decorum: You acted one way around women, another way around men. At a reception, one senator described somebody as a "no good son-of-a-bitch" only to realize suddenly, to his embarrassment, that Jordan was there. Jordan put him quickly at ease: "If a person is a no good son-of-a-bitch, then he's a no good son-of-a-bitch," she said to him.[7]

She sought out the most powerful members of the Senate, no matter how bigoted they were. Senator Aiken had never treated a black person as an equal, but she visited with him to show him her respect. Aiken had been the chief sponsor of a law that had significantly increased funding for public schools in Texas, so Jordan praised his efforts. Her actions began to build a camaraderie between the two of them.

Most importantly, she cultivated a relationship with Dorsey Hardeman, the archconservative. Even if Hardeman had proclaimed that he would take no orders from a black woman, Jordan knew he was perhaps the most powerful person in the Texas State Senate, a brilliant manipulator of its rules and procedures. She believed that she could learn from him.[8]

She began to study Hardeman's tactics, and when he noticed her imitating his parliamentary procedures, she told him she was trying to honor him. "I'm using the trickster's tricks," she said.[9] She began visiting Hardeman's office regularly for an afternoon drink. Jordan liked to tell the story of a liberal member of the Texas House who dropped by to visit her one afternoon. He was stunned to find her in Hardeman's office with Senators Aiken and Hardeman, a drink of scotch in her hand, her feet propped up on a chair.[10]

Jordan effectively appealed to Hardeman's vanity. She played student to his teacher, and Hardeman, who believed himself a gentleman, decided that she was smart and deserving of his lessons. He also decided that he liked her. In time, the racist senator became like a mentor to her even if they didn't vote the same way.

From her friendship with Hardeman, Jordan learned how to get a law passed and also how to prevent one from getting through the Texas Senate. While she often voted with the liberals, she knew where the true power of the Senate was, so she tried to be personally appealing to those conservative senators without being fake. Quick-witted, articulate, and amusing, she made the "good old boys" feel comfortable around her. She still was not admitted to some of the whites-only clubs of Austin or even the Astro club at the Astrodome back in Houston.[11] But Jordan actively socialized with the other senators as a matter of business. At the same time, the conservatives and all the other senators quickly recognized that Jordan was a person of formidable intelligence and growing popular appeal. Soon Jordan became the first woman ever invited to Senator Charles Wilson's annual quail hunt.[12]

Jordan did not speak on the Senate floor for nearly two months, all the while watching and learning. In fact, members of her district back in Houston became impatient that she was not speaking out for them. Then, in the middle of a debate on a proposed city sales tax, she rose. Like the liberals, she opposed strongly the sales tax because she believed that it was a regressive tax. A graduated income tax varied tax levels according to the wealth of individuals. It distributed the tax burden according to the ability to pay. A sales tax, however, took as much money from the poor as it did from the wealthy. It shifted the burden for funding the government toward those who could least afford it.

"Texas is number one in poor people because of its regressive tax structure," Jordan declared. "The poor people of this state pay approximately thirty per cent of their income in taxes. Where is the equity when the people who make the most pay the least, and the people who make the least pay the most?"[13]

Jordan's speech was specific and impassioned. It was a clear expression of the interests of her constituents, and it showed the liberals that she shared their ideals. But the conservatives, led by Hardeman, passed the tax bill. In fact, from the beginning of the debate, the conservatives knew they had the votes to do so. Dorsey Hardeman later explained that he did not mind Jordan opposing him in this debate because it had no effect on the passing of the law.[14] In her first speech, the best Jordan could do was to express the interests of her district and declare her beliefs. She managed to do so without antagonizing the leadership of the Texas Senate.

That may seem like a small victory, but Jordan's ability to speak out without creating more opposition to her was important. It had a long-range effect. Her constituents and the rest of the public were watching her. The newspapers carefully covered this first speech by the new, black state senator. To them, Jordan appeared a dedicated and principled defender of the poor. She appeared intelligent, articulate, and dynamic. Her first speech was helpful to her because it strengthened her appeal in her district, and it added to her popularity among the more liberal-minded elsewhere.

With her greater popularity came increased political power. Slowly, therefore, Jordan used her position to build goodwill among fellow legislators and to make her position as state senator into a kind of bully pulpit, from which she could speak out for the will of her constituents and her ideals.

Jordan was shrewd and determined. She had planned her way to Girl of the Year in high school; she had fought her way to state senator. Now she executed her strategy in the Texas Senate. For the moment, she spoke out selectively but with clear dedication to her beliefs. On the same day as the city tax bill debate, she addressed an audience of migrant farmworkers. She was cosponsoring a bill to establish a state minimum wage: "You've been waiting a long time to get a fair wage in Texas," she told the crowd. "This minimum wage is just going to be the start of a great, new movement."[15] The workers, mostly Mexican Americans, cheered and remembered her, enhancing her status as the most powerful black leader in the state. The bill, however, was defeated that year.

Jordan was engaged in a balancing act. She wanted to please her supporters, but she also needed to be effective. Quietly, behind closed doors and within the political system of the Texas Senate, she was finding a way to maximize her effect. To do that, she believed strongly that she must become a political insider no matter how others might criticize her. At times, she appeared less of an ally to other African American politicians than she believed she was. She was careful to separate herself from anyone that her conservative colleagues might consider an outsider or a disruptive force.

She did that even if it meant criticizing some of the most effective black leaders in the country. She said that she wanted the other senators "to know I was coming to be a senator, and I wasn't coming to lead any charge. I was not coming carrying the flag and singing 'We Shall Overcome'"—a song strongly identified with the civil-rights movement.[16] In effect, Jordan was distancing herself from civil-rights activists, whose goals and beliefs she shared. Yet Jordan believed that she could be effective only if she could form a personal relationship with her fellow senators; protesting, she thought, accomplished nothing.[17] As an insider in the Senate she believed that she could build a working relationship with most of the senators. Then, at selective moments, she could appeal to their "fairness and reasonableness."[18] That way, she believed that she could get something done for African Americans and for the poor.

She did not like to be criticized, especially by those who shared her beliefs but disagreed with her tactics. She was impatient with them, and she could be intimidating if necessary. A liberal state representative questioned how she could become so friendly with Hardeman and other conservatives. She answered him angrily, "They have the votes."[19] The message of her words was clear: Don't dare to question her strategy. She wasn't going to waste her time complaining about the racism of her colleagues. Whatever feelings of anger or frustration she felt about the good old boys in the Texas Senate, she kept those feelings private.

The job as state senator paid little, so Jordan was forced to continue her law practice in Houston. She worked hard and found herself under enormous pressure. It seemed as if she was always standing in the spotlight of her constituents, always living up to the expectations of her family, or always politicking with other senators. She needed a life apart from all that, especially "out in the white world" of Austin. She made friends with a small circle of women, some of whom became lifelong companions. Anne Appenzellar, Betty Whitaker, Caroline Dowell, and Nancy Earl were people who did not want any political favor from her and were wholly trustworthy.

Jordan had found a place to live on Norwalk Lane in Austin, the same neighborhood as Appenzellar, whom she had met at the YWCA. Through Appenzellar, she met Whitaker. Soon they were barbecuing together, and finally they went on a camping and fishing trip to Inks Lake. Eventually, through them, Jordan met Nancy Earl at a gathering by a campground where Betty Whitaker had bought a trailer. Jordan immediately liked Earl in particular. Together, they ate, drank, and threw parties. Often, they brought guitars and sang together. Jordan's specialty was blues songs. Anne Appenzellar and especially Nancy Earl became loyal friends and frequent companions. For the first time since arriving in Austin, Jordan felt that she was among people with whom she could relax.[20]

Meanwhile, her strategy in the Texas Senate appeared to work. During her first term, she successfully blocked passage of a bill from the conservatives that would have made it significantly more difficult for voters to register. Since the late nineteenth century, inhibiting voter registration had been a favorite tactic for decreasing black voting power. Jordan also blocked one of two competing state budget bills because the bill came from Governor John Connally, who had opposed ending segregation in public places.[21]

At the end of her first year, her fellow senators voted her Outstanding Freshman Senator. It was an astonishing change over the course of a single session. Jordan believed most of the senators now admired her, even if they didn't like her. She responded by telling them that they had begun the year "with suspicion, fear, and apprehension"; now, however, she called each of them "friend."[22]

9 New Friends in High Places

Most of the Texas state senators recognized that Barbara Jordan was quickly becoming someone with whom they needed to cultivate a relationship. Jordan was new and different for the Texas Senate. As a result, she attracted frequent press attention. That made it more difficult for conservatives to oppose her without their receiving bad publicity. In March 1967, she presided over a Senate session for fifteen minutes, a routine that all senators performed. Yet she was the first black woman to do so. It made headline news in a Dallas newspaper and received coverage on nearly all Texas television stations. The Associated Press distributed a photo of her with the Senate gavel in her hand, so her photograph was published in newspapers nationwide.[1] At the end of her first term, in 1968, she was named one of the ten most influential women in Texas—an astonishing recognition for a black woman in the state.[2]

Meanwhile, Jordan had received even more significant attention only one month after she assumed office.

*Jordan at 1967 discussions on fair housing
legislation in Washington, D.C.*

In February 1967, President Lyndon Johnson invited her to counsel him on fair-housing legislation proposals. Johnson wanted the integration of housing to be the next great initiative in the civil-rights movement. To Jordan's surprise, Johnson contacted her, asking her to fly to Washington to advise him. There she met with President Johnson, Vice President Hubert Humphrey, and Attorney General Ramsey Clark, as well as some of the leading civil-rights leaders of the United States.[3] Roy Wilkins, executive secretary of the NAACP; Whitney Young, director of the Urban League; and Dorothy Height, president of the National Council of Negro Women, were among them.

That meeting was a dizzying experience for Jordan. There she was, invited by her president to attend a meeting with some of the most powerful people in the nation. She was ambitious, but she knew that she did not have the political stature of the other people in the room. As she listened to President Johnson outline his proposed fair housing bill, she was uncertain whether or not the president knew who she was. Then Johnson finished his presentation and said, "Now let's hear from some of you." He turned to Jordan: "Barbara, what do you think of this?"[4] Jordan was stunned. She stuttered out an answer: It was probably a good time for such legislation, although it would be an uphill battle. She barely remembered the rest of the meeting. When it ended, she quickly returned to Texas.

From all the signs, however, it appeared that she had gained the favor of the president. In *The Washington Post* the following day, a political column reported that "the White House was far more impressed with her than the usual run of civil-rights leaders."[5]

Intelligent and dedicated, Jordan was an appealing person for Lyndon Johnson. She was also lucky enough to be in the right place at the right time. President Johnson's circumstances made Barbara Jordan an attractive ally for him. Jordan had been elected at a difficult and vulnerable time in Johnson's presidency. Johnson was a man of enormous drive and ambition. Born into poverty in the Texas hill country, he had been elected a congressman, then a senator, and then vice president under John F. Kennedy in 1960. When Kennedy was assassinated in 1963, he took over the presidency and then was elected to the office in 1964. Along the way he had built a reputation as fierce, combative, and even ruthless in pursuit of his ambitions.

Once he became president, however, Johnson showed that he was deeply concerned about the legacy he would leave behind him when he retired. He was sensitive to any challenge to his reputation, and he was determined to be remembered as someone who bettered society.[6] After criticism by civil-rights leaders and the press, he strongly supported the Civil Rights Act of 1964 and the Voting Rights Act of 1965. Johnson had twisted arms and otherwise rallied politicians behind the bills until they were passed, in spite of the silent and not-so-silent objections of southern Democrats.

This was a remarkable transformation for Johnson. When he was a congressman from 1937 to 1948, Johnson had voted against every civil-rights bill. He voted against integrating the armed forces, and he even voted against an antilynching law. (The lynching of African Americans by white vigilante groups had been a widespread form of murder in the South since the turn of the century.) Running for the Senate in 1948, Johnson had attacked President Harry Truman's civil-rights initiative. Once elected to the Senate, Johnson was the youngest ally of an older group of conservative, southern senators that included die-hard segregationists such as James Eastland of Mississippi.[7]

Then Lyndon Johnson changed. As president, he was under the scrutiny of the entire country. He wanted to be remembered as a president who had made a difference in the lives of all Americans, and he worried deeply, to the point of obsession, that his reputation might be anything different. Under pressure from civil-rights leaders, he pushed through the Civil Rights Act of 1964, which some people call the most significant civil-rights legislation of the twentieth century. He did not want to pursue a voting-rights law. But then civil-rights leaders and the press criticized him for not protecting the right of black citizens to vote in the South. He changed his mind, an about-face that led to the Voting Rights Act of 1965.

That law provided the federal government with the right to oversee state and local elections in the Deep South. It authorized the federal government to ensure that African Americans could freely register to vote and to gain access to the polls. Texas, however, was mostly excluded from the jurisdiction of the law. But the law was a vital tool for African Americans to gain political power. And Johnson used the power of the presidency to encourage their advancement. Speaking to Congress, Johnson declared that the cause of African Americans "must be our cause, too. Because it is not just Negroes, but really it is all of us, who must overcome the crippling legacy of bigotry and injustice." Later he called the Voting Rights Act his "greatest accomplishment."[8] Johnson had come a long way from his days as a congressman.

But because of his past actions, civil-rights leaders still did not fully trust him. And Johnson, at the time Barbara Jordan was invited to the White House, badly wanted public appreciation for his stance on civil rights. Recently, he had been attacked for his actions in Vietnam, and those attacks had become increasingly severe.

In 1965, Johnson had ordered the first fighting troops into Vietnam. He told the public he was not doing so. He also promised that he would not widen the war. Until April 1965, there had been only 16,000 American troops in Vietnam. All of them were non-combatants advising the South Vietnamese in their civil war against communists in North Vietnam. Four months after his promise, Johnson increased the United States force in Vietnam to 219,000 fighting soldiers. By the end of 1966, shortly before Barbara Jordan took office, more than 16,000 Americans had lost their lives in Vietnam.[9]

The casualties and America's greater involvement in Vietnam produced a massive uprising against the war and against Lyndon Johnson. In gatherings across the country and on the television news, Johnson heard protesters chanting, "Hey, hey, LBJ! How many kids did you kill today?"[10] It tortured Johnson to think that he might be remembered in such a way. Because of the war and increased opposition to him, Johnson did not run for a second term as president in 1968. But he was powerfully concerned about his public reputation at all times.

His civil-rights legacy became increasingly important to him. In 1966 and 1967, he was under criticism and pressure to desegregate the nation still more thoroughly. Martin Luther King took his movement north to Chicago, where he tried to integrate housing. A younger generation of leaders, including Stokely Carmichael of the Student Nonviolent Coordinating Committee (SNCC) and Floyd McKissick of the Congress of Racial Equality (CORE), were much more outspoken and confrontational than Johnson would tolerate.

Lyndon Johnson felt as if his entire legacy as a president was going to be ruined by the criticism against him. When he invited Jordan to the White House, Johnson still harbored hope for his civil-rights record. He was searching for new, young leaders among African Americans—people with whom he could not simply build legislation but divert attention from civil-rights leaders he considered too radical and too critical of him. King was invited to the meeting, but he declined. Carmichael and McKissick were not invited.[11]

Johnson quickly decided that he liked Jordan because he felt a common bond with her. Both of them cultivated a no-nonsense style of speaking. Both could be imposing, even intimidating. Both came from humble backgrounds in Texas.

In turn, Barbara Jordan was awed and grateful for Johnson's attention. She believed in Johnson's commitment to civil rights. It was typical of Jordan that she would feel people can and would change. She thought that in their hearts, people were reasonable if someone would make a personal appeal to them. In Johnson, she saw someone whom she believed had become genuinely and passionately dedicated to civil rights. She had also made a powerful friend, and she knew it. So did her colleagues in the Texas Senate.

Barbara Jordan's first term in the Texas Senate lasted only two years because the 1966 redistricting came in the middle of a legislative term. In 1968 she was easily reelected, this time for four years. By then, Jordan was virtually an insider in Austin and she had gained enough power to become remarkably successful in such a conservative political body. In her two terms in the Texas Senate, more than half of the bills Barbara Jordan sponsored became law. With the liberal bloc of senators, she fulfilled her promise to migrant workers by maneuvering the state's first minimum-wage law through the Senate. She pushed through a law to increase worker's compensation benefits—money paid out when a worker is injured on the job.[12] She sponsored a law that established the Texas Fair Employment Practices Commission. She showed a consistent commitment to organized labor, the poor, and the working poor. Along with Frances "Sissy" Farenthold, elected during Jordan's second term in the Texas Senate, Jordan sponsored the ratification of the federal Equal Rights Amendment in Texas and saw through passage of the Equal Legal Rights Amendment to the Texas Constitution.[13]

Jordan readily admitted that some of her legislation had "gums but no teeth" to enforce its provisions.[14] Yet she had helped to change the political landscape of the Texas Senate. Liberals, she declared, had more power than ever before.[15] Her popularity in Texas and with the Democratic party grew.

At Lyndon Johnson's request, she introduced him when he spoke before a fund-raiser for the reelection campaign of U.S. Senator Ralph Yarborough. Once again, Jordan showed her stunning ability to capture the attention and build the enthusiasm of an audience. Johnson thought her introduction was the best he had ever been given. Grateful and impressed, he told her that he was going to help her political career "in whatever way I can."[16]

The national Democratic party noticed Jordan. Houston lawyer Robert Strauss was powerful in the Democratic National Committee. Eventually he would become its chairman. At his invitation, Jordan flew to Miami to participate in a fund-raiser, where she posed for photographs with Ted Kennedy. That only increased her visibility as a rising star in state and national politics.[17]

But politics sometimes demanded that she make some sacrifices. Jordan soon attracted powerful Democratic supporters within Texas who were eager to advance her career. But their help forced her to give up on some political positions she appeared to believe in.

When she first became a senator, Jordan had called for distributing the money for Texas state universities more fairly. The University of Texas had collected a vast amount of money in its "Permanent University Fund." Jordan wanted schools such as Texas Southern to receive their fair share of it. But she abandoned that position once she gained the political support of Frank Erwin, a powerful Democrat and the chairman of the University of Texas Board of Regents. In turn, Erwin had been one of the people who brought Jordan to Lyndon Johnson's attention.[18]

Loyalty, too, led her to make compromises. As a Texas delegate to the 1968 Democratic convention in Chicago, she voted to support Lyndon Johnson's policies on Vietnam, in spite of her doubts about the war. From the day he invited her to the White House and recognized her at the meeting, Johnson had her unqualified support. She couldn't bring herself to vote against him.[19]

These compromises led to her gaining still greater support from the political establishment. That in turn launched the next stage in her political career. After the 1970 census, the number of seats for the United States House of Representatives was adjusted for each state. Because the population of Texas had grown, the state earned an additional congressional seat beginning with the 1972 elections.

From his ranch near Austin, where he had retired, Lyndon Johnson let it be known that he wanted that new seat to cover a district around Houston, for Barbara Jordan. Another ally, Lieutenant Governor Ben Barnes, made Barbara Jordan vice chair of the committee that drew up the boundaries for the new districts.[20] When the work of the committee was done, the population of the new 18th Congressional District was more than half African American. An additional quarter of its constituents were Mexican American.[21] They would strongly support her candidacy for Congress.

Then the Democratic political establishment of Houston turned out to support her. In October 1971, Jordan held a gala fund-raiser for her congressional campaign. The event was in downtown Houston, a difference from the more modest surroundings of the Fifth Ward. Looking at the 1,500 people who attended, Jordan could see a change had occurred. Her supporters included more than the constituents of her district. There were stockbrokers, bankers, and other financial backers of the Democratic party. Even the conservative mayor, Louie Welch, attended

In the midst of the party, former president Lyndon Johnson arrived, as he had promised. Johnson was ailing; he had already suffered a heart attack. Yet his commitment to Jordan was strong. With Jordan at his side, the old pro worked the room, shaking the hands of all the partygoers, making it known that Jordan was indeed the anointed one, the favored candidate of the Democratic party.[22] Then Johnson stepped up to the speakers' platform and addressed the crowd. Gushing with emotion, he said that he endorsed Barbara Jordan with all his heart. She was more than a good candidate for Congress. She was living proof that a new, more inclusive political order was rising in America. "Barbara Jordan proved to us that black is beautiful before we knew what that meant," he said. "She is a woman of keen intellect and unusual legislative ability. . . . Those with hurting consciences because they have discriminated against blacks and women can vote for Barbara Jordan and feel good."[23]

Johnson's speech made a vote for Jordan appear to be a way of easing the guilt of those who had wronged African Americans in the past. He asked the audience to think of Jordan as a symbol that African Americans in Texas could overcome racial barriers. It was the same kind of symbol Barbara Jordan would make of herself four years later, when she was the keynote speaker at the Democratic National Convention in New York. The fund-raiser and Johnson's support were successful. In the fall of 1972, the major daily newspapers of Houston endorsed an African American for Congress for the first time.[24]

While Jordan's election was virtually guaranteed, a painful controversy developed. Curtis Graves challenged her in the primary. Graves was the African American elected state representative when Jordan first became state senator. His district overlapped Jordan's district for the Texas Senate, and he had hoped to move up to her seat. But Jordan's senatorial district had vanished when the new legislative districts were established. Graves blamed Jordan.[25]

Barbara Jordan was vice chair of the redistricting committee that had overseen the creation of the Congressional district she now sought to represent. But she had let other senators and appointees take over the redistricting plans once that district was established. Conservatives quickly redrew the state legislative districts so that Graves would not be elected. They knew Graves to be a more confrontational politician, a veteran of the Houston sit-in movement of 1960. So the conservatives made sure he had no chance of entering the Texas Senate. Effectively, they eliminated the possibility that an African American would be elected senator in Harris County. Once Barbara Jordan was gone, the Senate would return to its status as an all-white club.[26]

Graves was outraged. In spite of her commitment to equality for African Americans, Jordan had not supported his political ambitions. He charged that Jordan had sacrificed his seat in the Texas Senate to advance her own career in the United States Congress.

Graves sued the state of Texas in federal court. He charged that the new legislative districts diluted black voting power. Called to testify in the case, Barbara Jordan felt disturbed and guilty for what had happened. In a deposition, she said that Graves was partly right. No black would be elected state senator from the new Eleventh District.[27] But she insisted that the new legislative districts did not intentionally reduce the voting strength of African Americans. The court ruled against Graves.

So Graves decided to run for Congress. He hadn't a chance of winning, but he made it clear that he considered Jordan a sellout. He denounced her as the "Aunt Jemima of Texas politics." In the May 1972 Democratic primary, Barbara Jordan trounced Graves. She received 80 percent of the popular vote and 90 percent of the African American vote.[28]

Once the Texas senators were sure that Jordan would be leaving them, they honored her. Jordan's fellow senators decided to make her Governor for a Day on June 10, 1972. This was a tradition peculiar to the Texas Senate. By electing her president pro tem of the Senate, they made her third in command to the governor, behind the lieutenant governor. Then the governor and lieutenant governor left the state for a day. Although it was largely ceremonial, the appointment was truly important to Jordan and her supporters in her district. For the first time in Texas history, a black woman became governor of Texas.[29] Jordan wanted her constituents to participate, so she invited all the schoolchildren of her district as well as the school bands from Phillis Wheatley and Jack Yates High Schools.

For her family and herself that day, Jordan rented a suite in a hotel. Then they had breakfast in the governor's mansion, after which they attended a ceremony in the Senate chamber, where she was sworn in as governor. For a moment unlike any in her political career, it appeared as if African Americans dominated the Texas capitol. There were so many people from her district in the senate gallery, that Jordan thought it was "blacked out."[30] Someone took down the Confederate flag from the statehouse.

But it was a bittersweet celebration. In the midst of the reception, Ben Jordan collapsed with a stroke and was rushed by ambulance to a nearby hospital. For

Texas Governor for the Day, Barbara Jordan

some time before the event, Ben Jordan had suffered from serious heart problems, but he refused to miss his daughter's day of honor.

Her father's illness made Barbara Jordan feel both concerned and troubled. In the years since she had returned from Boston, she had lost respect for him. She had no patience for his stern attempts to command his family. Then, one night, she discovered that the Reverend Ben Jordan had secretly been having an affair with another woman. Angry and hurt, Jordan never said a word to him or to her mother. But the emotional ties that bound her to him were gone, she felt.[31]

Yet she remained a dutiful daughter. That evening, she visited her father in the hospital before attending a party in her honor. In the middle of it, she was called back to the hospital. Barbara, Bennie, and Rose Mary joined Arlyne, who had been there since his arrival. Before them, Ben Jordan slipped into a coma.

It was late, but Barbara felt this was still a special day. She was distant enough from her father that she would not let his condition stop her from celebrating. She found Nancy Earl and her other good friends. They returned to her hotel suite with a guitar and held a private party until morning, when the hospital called to say that Ben Jordan was dying. Barbara returned to the hospital in time to be with her father when he died.[32]

Although she had lost her strong attachment to her father, Jordan still felt his death powerfully. Ben Jordan had been an enormous presence in her life, someone she had battled against and learned from for more than thirty-six years. He had taught her discipline. He had urged her to be ambitious, and he had paid her way through college and law school. Barbara comforted herself with the thought that this was probably the day her father would have chosen to die.

Five months later, in November 1972, she beat her Republican opponent by a landslide. She was the newly elected United States congresswoman from the Eighteenth Congressional District of Texas.

10 *Of*
Washington D.C. and Watergate

In January 1973, Barbara Jordan was sworn in as the first black woman from the South and the first Texas woman in the United States Congress. She and Andrew Young of Georgia were the first two African Americans to represent the South since Reconstruction. The media wanted interviews with her. The Democratic National Committee wanted to use her as a symbol of their support for civil rights.

Jordan, however, was more interested in learning how to be effective in Congress. She was there to represent her constituents, who now numbered 500,000. She wanted to speak out for the ideals she believed in and the changes she sought to make in the politics of the United States. Those ideals were the same she pursued in the Texas Senate: abolishing all forms of racial discrimination; creating a more compassionate, open society for the poor and powerless; and guaranteeing that all citizens could equally and fully participate in the political process.

All high-minded principles aside, her strategy was to become an insider, just as she had been in the Texas Senate. She set about her work. From an experienced congressional staff member, she learned practical tips on how to select a staff and which committees in Congress might be desirable. Jordan quickly was attracted to the Judiciary Committee.[1]

Meanwhile, the Congressional Black Caucus, the coalition of African Americans in Congress, asked her to join the Armed Services Committee, where no African American was assigned. There were already two—John Conyers of Michigan and Charles Rangel of New York—on the Judiciary Committee. Both Armed Services and Judiciary were considered "major committees"; Jordan would be able to serve on only one of them.

Jordan wrote Lyndon Johnson for his advice and promptly received a phone call. Johnson told her to choose the Judiciary Committee. It was less controversial, the former president told her, and it might pave the way for her becoming a federal judge, if she should ever want to be one. Johnson had already called the person in charge of committee assignments, the powerful head of the Ways and Means Committee, Wilbur Mills. Mills agreed to do as Lyndon Johnson asked. So Jordan bucked the Congressional Black Caucus on this matter and chose the Judiciary Committee.[2]

In Washington, Jordan quickly found an experienced administrative assistant to head her office. She wanted as much help becoming an insider in Washington as she could, so she left her staff from Texas in Houston and found Rufus "Bud" Myers to head her staff. Bud Myers was an experienced congressional staff member. He was also black, which Jordan thought would "satisfy" both her colleagues and her constituents' desires for still more African Americans on Capitol Hill.[3] Most importantly, she believed that she could trust him.

Her move to Washington meant that she suddenly found herself working with 435 representatives, an increase of more than 400 people over the Texas Senate. In the past, her political style had been to cultivate personal relationships with all her colleagues. Now she was in so large a political body that it became necessary to build alliances and work with existing groups within Congress.

The Congressional Black Caucus was one such group. The year Jordan entered Congress, the House of Representatives included more African Americans than at any other time in the twentieth century. Of the fifteen members of the Black Caucus, three were women—Shirley Chisholm of Brooklyn, New York; Yvonne Burke of Los Angeles; and Jordan. The caucus members became important allies for many pieces of legislation.[4]

Her first priority, however, was the Texas congressional delegation, one of the most powerful groups within Congress. Texans held no fewer than six major committee chairmanships, including that of the House Democratic Caucus.

Among her fellow Texans, she acted as she would in the Texas Senate, forming personal relationships with delegation members. She actively courted them, no matter what their political convictions were. It made her immediately successful. Before Jordan, no woman had been allowed to attend the weekly luncheon hosted by the Texas Democratic delegation. With Jordan's arrival, that tradition changed quickly.[5]

Jordan was an imposing and intriguing politician to the other members of the Texas delegation. Her dark skin contrasted with the appearance of most of the delegation. Her size made her look powerful, and her voice, always forceful and dynamic, made her presence all the more dramatic. A lobbyist from Texas commented that she looked "like she might be God, if God turns out to be a black woman."[6] With the attention she received from the Democrat National Committee and from the media, the Texas delegation knew immediately that she would be a figure to be reckoned with. They elected her secretary of the delegation.

Jordan's final preparation before the term began was to select a seat on the floor of the House of Representatives. She showed her independence when she chose a location on the center aisle rather than next to the Congressional Black Caucus members and liberals. Her choice, she said, was wholly practical: She would be directly in the line of sight of the Speaker of the House, Thomas "Tip" O'Neill.

But her location also sent out another message. She wanted to chart her own path. She would vote liberal, and she would strongly support the interests of African Americans. But she would not be pigeonholed. She wanted to become an insider in Washington, too. For that, she needed to appear to be her own person to the conservatives in Congress, especially to the Texas delegation.[7]

At her swearing in on January 3, 1973, Jordan was surrounded by the Texas congressional delegation while her family and friends looked on.[8] Jordan would have gone immediately to work if Lyndon Johnson had not suddenly died. Grieving, Jordan spoke from the floor of the House. She declared Lyndon Johnson her mentor and friend. She spoke of her love for him and her belief in his essential "concern for people": "Old men straightened their stooped backs because Lyndon Johnson lived; little children dared look forward to intellectual achievement because he lived; black Americans became excited about a future of opportunity, hope, justice, and dignity."[9] Whatever mixed sentiments existed in the nation about Lyndon Johnson, Jordan showed once again that she was grateful and fiercely loyal to him. She insisted that people remember him as a powerful, constructive force in the country.

Jordan's life as a congresswoman in Washington, D.C., was nearly all business. She worked twelve hours

Jordan with Johnson at the Lyndon Baines Johnson Library in 1972

a day at the office and still more at home. She felt constantly as though she needed to work harder because others were better prepared than she was. Because of that, she insisted that her staff make her an expert in whatever matter she was addressing in committee or on the floor of the House.[10] When she wasn't writing bills or preparing herself for committee meetings, she cultivated relationships with the most powerful members of Congress.

The demands of her position aside, her job gave her more than enough money for the first time in her life.[11] She didn't have to continue her law practice. It felt somehow unreal to be making good money. At first, she would stuff her billfold with hundred-dollar bills, just so she could peek at all the money. She never spent it. (Her family constantly told her that she was too tight with money.) Eventually, the novelty wore off, and she awoke to the risks of carrying around so much cash.[12]

Jordan may have been unconfident about her preparation for Congress, but she was unusually successful in a short period of time. Her experience in the Texas Senate had taught her well. She was unafraid to speak directly with conservative members of Congress about her push for expanding civil-rights legislation. But she was shrewd enough not to confront them. Most of all, she impressed conservatives and nearly everyone else as not only straightforward but remarkably intelligent and well versed in whatever subject she addressed.[13]

As she pursued civil-rights legislation, she convinced many and humbled others. Congressman George Mahon was the conservative chair of the House Appropriations Committee. He declared that in his forty years in Congress he had never seen anyone "capture so quickly the response of the House."[14]

She displayed that ability repeatedly during her first term, especially where her efforts could attack racial discrimination. She successfully added a civil-rights provision to a crime control bill. That provision came to be known as the Jordan Amendment, and it meant that federal money used for law enforcement, prisons, and crime-prevention programs had to be used in a nondiscriminatory way. Federal money was essential to the funding of police departments across the country. The result of her amendment, Jordan hoped, would be that Houston and other city police forces would finally hire a reasonable number of African Americans.

To get her amendment through both houses of Congress, Jordan had to convince Senator John McClellan, a conservative from Arkansas. McClellan chaired the House-Senate conference committee that met to reconcile their two versions of the bill. Jordan got herself appointed to that conference committee. Then she simply sat beside McClellan throughout the meetings and forced the committee to consider her amendment. Every time McClellan raised an objection, she answered him politely and firmly until, in the end, he agreed.[15]

Yet the chief drama during her first two years—the one that first brought her to the attention of ordinary citizens across the nation—was a conflict with President Richard Nixon. Her assignment to the Judiciary Committee placed her amidst one of the most significant political events in the history of the country, which began seven months before she was elected.

On June 17, 1972, Washington, D.C., police arrested five men burglarizing the Democratic National Committee headquarters in the Watergate office building.

Each of the men wore business suits and rubber surgical gloves. With them they had walkie-talkies, forty rolls of unexposed photography film, and bugging devices. They carried more than $2,200, most of it in crisp, new, hundred-dollar bills, their serial numbers in sequence. One of them, James McCord Jr., was an ex-FBI agent and former head of physical security for the CIA. He was also a full-time employee of the Committee for the Re-Election of the President, Richard M. Nixon.

The burglary had all the signs of a crime financed and organized by employees of the president. Its goal appeared to be spying upon and thereby subverting the political campaign of his Democratic opponent in the coming election.[16] In the fall of 1972, when Nixon was reelected, the investigation of the crime had only begun.

By the end of 1973, however, it had led to full-scale hearings in the United States Senate and to the appointment of a special independent prosecutor. The attorney general of the United States and twelve other top officials in the Nixon administration had resigned.[17] From the Senate Watergate hearings, it became increasingly clear that the Watergate burglary was one of several illegal operations that the president's reelection committee had financed and organized. Employees of the FBI, the CIA, and the IRS had committed a series of crimes against political opponents of President Nixon, from illegal wiretaps to break-ins to tax harassment. Investigators suspected and later confirmed that President Nixon himself knew of these illegal activities; and he knew of the Watergate burglary within one week of its occurrence.

With the help of his closest advisors, President Nixon plotted a cover-up operation to prevent any connection between the burglars and his campaign. When that failed, President Nixon and his men tried to prevent anyone from tracing the illegal activities back to his closest advisors and to himself. They stonewalled the investigator, and they fired the special independent prosecutor, Archibald Cox, in October 1973. They replaced Cox with Barbara Jordan's Houston colleague Leon Jaworski. (That firing came to be known as the "Saturday Night Massacre." The new attorney general, Elliott Richardson, resigned rather than fire Cox as ordered. Solicitor General Robert Bork agreed to do it.) Along the way, many of the president's closest advisors resigned. Some had been indicted or, in exchange for immunity, revealed what they knew about these crimes.

The Nixon administration was in crisis, but the crisis got worse. Over the course of his presidency, Richard Nixon had taped all of his conversations in the Oval Office of the White House. He had kept his tapes. Once the existence of the tapes was uncovered, the independent prosecutor wanted them for his investigation. Eventually, the Supreme Court ruled that "the White House tapes" did not belong to President Nixon and must be submitted as evidence to the independent prosecutor and to investigating committees within Congress.

President Nixon stalled handing over the tapes as long as he could. The tapes would confirm that he had obstructed justice in the Watergate affair and had full knowledge of many of the other crimes. He handed over only censored and partial transcripts of some of the tapes. Slowly, however, he was forced to release more of the tapes. Their contents were highly damaging to the president. By February 1974, the House of

Representatives authorized its Judiciary Committee to investigate whether or not Richard Nixon should be impeached. The chair of that committee was Congressman Peter Rodino of New Jersey.

The political leadership of the nation was in turmoil. The government was absorbed in the drama of the president and his men. As if this were not enough, Vice President Spiro Agnew had resigned in October 1973 because he was under investigation for bribery, tax fraud, and extortion. In Agnew's place, Representative Gerald Ford of Michigan was confirmed as vice president.

Barbara Jordan had heard the calls for Nixon's impeachment since the middle of 1973, but she did not believe it could happen. Then, when the Supreme Court ordered the White House to hand over the tapes, she changed her mind.[18] For five months, from February into July, the Judiciary Committee met behind closed doors to debate what charges might be brought against the president that qualified for impeachment. The Constitution declared that a president could only be removed from office for "treason, bribery, or other high crimes and misdemeanors."

Jordan was glad the committee met behind closed doors because they were discussing the character of the president. Jordan felt an immense responsibility. The office of the president was virtually unable to function until this issue was resolved. The media and seemingly the entire nation was focused on the event. Each day, when she emerged through the doors of the Judiciary Committee meeting room, she was overwhelmed by reporters shouting questions.[19]

Her response to them was silence. Her duty, she believed, was to be secret about their deliberations. She never spoke about them with her staff or with friends. She never offered an opinion about Richard Nixon's guilt or innocence. She rarely spoke in the closed-door meetings.[20]

Instead, she listened to the evidence and plunged herself into research on the Constitution. She felt as if her duties as a representative had changed. She no longer had time to serve the immediate interests of her Congressional district. Instead, her focus was to assess the case against Nixon and to interpret the meaning of impeachment in the Constitution. She investigated every impeachment case she could find and every statement on impeachment by the writers and framers of the Constitution. She consulted with Senator Sam Ervin, chairman of the Senate Watergate Committee and a noted constitutional scholar. She even visited the National Archives twice, simply to stare at the 200-year-old document and the Bill of Rights.[21]

In late July 1974, the thirty-five-member Judiciary Committee emerged from its closed sessions. It televised hearings of its final deliberations. Publicly, the committee members would discuss whether or not they should create articles of impeachment. The nation watched. After five months, Jordan had heard enough to make up her mind. The president, she thought, should undoubtedly be impeached for obstruction of justice and for violation of the constitutional rights of other citizens. But she wanted the committee to discuss the matter immediately, and then to vote. She was nearly alone in her opinion. Her colleagues wanted each of them first to make a fifteen-minute speech. Then they would deliberate.[22]

Jordan urged her colleagues to hold a discussion dominated by "reason and not passion."[23] Jordan

MR. EILBERG

MS. JORDAN

*Jordan and Charles Rangel look over a copy of the
Constitution during a House Judiciary Committee
debate on articles of impeachment for President
Nixon, July 26, 1974.*

thought speech making at that time would only lead to more politicking and less thoughtful conversation. But her colleagues on the committee felt that the newly opened hearings were an important, historical moment. Whether they were Republicans or Democrats, they could plead their case on television, before the nation as well as each other. Jordan was uncomfortable with the decision of the committee. She avoided thinking about her speech until the last moment.

Jordan was one of the last to speak. She was scheduled for an evening session of the committee on July 25. That afternoon, Bud Myers asked her what she was going to say. She still didn't know. At six P.M., she asked her secretary, Marian Ricks, to stay on while she began to work on a draft. Two and one-half hours later, Jordan walked into the committee room with several pages of notes her secretary had hastily typed as well as a list of President Nixon's actions. She began speaking at nine P.M., prime time for television viewers across the country.[24]

Jordan was exhausted by months of deliberation. She had also felt ill for months. By then, however, public speaking came easily to her. Her thoughts came together as she began to talk.

"Today I am an inquisitor," Jordan said. "I believe hyperbole would not be fictional and would not overstate the solemnness that I feel right now. My faith in the Constitution is whole. It is complete. It is total." She spoke emphatically, her voice rising.

"I am not going to sit here and be an idle spectator to the diminution, the subversion, the destruction of the Constitution."[25]

Jordan was only beginning her speech. She said that she and her fellow committee members were not assembled to remove the president from office. Instead, the Constitution dictated that for impeachment, they were the prosecutors of the case—"the accusers"; the senators would be the judges.

She reviewed the historical grounds for the impeachment of a president. She described impeachment as only justifiable, according to the framers of the Constitution, if a president has grown "swollen with power" and "tyrannical."

She believed that the crimes had to be so great that Congress was not divided according to political parties on the issue. "Common sense," she continued, "would be revolted if we engaged upon this process for petty reasons. Congress has a lot to do: appropriations, tax reform, health insurance, campaign finance reform, housing, environment protection. . . . "

But they were not being petty, Jordan said. She then listed what the president knew about Watergate and the crimes of which she believed he was guilty. She reminded her audience that James Madison, at the Constitutional Convention in 1787 said: "A President is impeachable if he attempts to subvert the Constitution." President Nixon, Jordan charged, "has counseled his aides to commit perjury, willfully disregarded the secrecy of grand jury proceedings," and more.

Then she summarized her argument. If President Nixon's actions aren't grounds for impeachment, she said, "then perhaps that eighteenth-century Constitution should be abandoned to a twentieth-century paper shredder."[26] When she finished, the committee was silent.

Jordan was not sure why they were silent until she left the Capitol that evening. At her car, however, the thirty-eight-year-old Jordan realized that she had inspired a nation. She was suddenly surrounded by a crowd of people screaming their approval of her. In the days that followed, hundreds of people who had heard her speech on television and radio called and wrote that they were inspired and gratified. They praised her for her eloquence, for the intelligence of her presentation, and for the extraordinary power of her voice. One couple wrote that for the first time they believed a black woman or man could be president. CBS News analyst Bruce Morton described her as "the best mind on the [Judiciary] committee."[27]

In the hearts and minds of her audience, Barbara Jordan's hastily prepared speech had transformed her into a symbol for upholding the Constitution. She was no longer simply a representative of Congress attending to the interests of her Houston constituents. She was a voice and a conscience within national politics.

Meanwhile, in those last days of July, the Judiciary Committee began to draft articles of impeachment. An important minority of conservative Democrats and Republicans were not yet convinced that Nixon should be impeached. They demanded there be specific, clear evidence of Nixon's wrongdoing. They repeatedly clashed with liberals on the committee, who were the majority. The conflict worried committee chairman Peter Rodino. He believed that whatever decisions the committee reached, it must be as bipartisan as possible. Within a short time, he recognized Barbara Jordan as a kind of informal mediator between the two opposing groups.

Her effort became easier within a matter of days. As they deliberated, the committee was still receiving White House tapes that the president had delayed sending. Each of those tapes proved more damaging to Nixon's case. Some of the Judiciary Committee members who were most reluctant to impeach changed their minds. Then, on July 27, the committee voted on the first article of impeachment. The room was nearly silent as they approved it, 27 to 11. Six Republicans voted with all twenty-one Democrats. Away from the cameras and the crowd of onlookers, Jordan, Rodino, and many of the other committee members broke into tears.[28]

In the next eight days, more White House tapes came in. The Judiciary Committee approved two more articles of impeachment and began to consider more. But they stopped their deliberations on August 8, 1974. President Richard Nixon resigned from office.

11 In and Out of the National Limelight

Barbara Jordan began a second term in Congress in January 1975. By then, she was a different politician. In the wake of her Judiciary Committee speech, her visibility to the nation and her ability as a speaker had made her more influential. Outside the House of Representatives, she was suddenly in demand. Requests poured in for her to speak from across the country. Old friends surfaced to ask special favors. From Ohio, Charles White, with whom she had walked home from Wheatley High School each afternoon, suddenly phoned with a request: Would she speak before a Planned Parenthood meeting? Issie Shelton, her Boston University Law School classmate, asked Jordan to dinner with other prominent blacks in Washington, D.C. Even Louise Bailey, who hadn't invited Jordan to her home for Christmas that first year in Boston, called with an invitation. Jordan raised her speaking fee and selected only a few engagements for causes she truly believed in.[1]

Meanwhile, she courted her fellow representatives and increased her stature in Congress. She made appearances at fund-raisers for Black Caucus members Ronald Dellums and Yvonne Burke of California. For women, she gave speeches to advocate the passage of the Equal Rights Amendment. And she gave weekly commentaries on topics of her choosing on *The CBS Morning News.*[2]

Her increased visibility led one of her colleagues to suggest that she run for the United States Senate. Texas senator Lloyd Bentsen proposed that she would be a fine candidate for the Supreme Court when a vacancy occurred in 1975. But Jordan did not agree with either of the suggestions. She was no constitutional scholar, she said, so the Supreme Court was not realistic. And she dismissed as impossible the idea of a black woman becoming senator from Texas.[3]

But she knew that she could be more effective in Congress, where public reaction to her role on the Judiciary Committee had made her more influential among fellow House members. Meanwhile, in the elections of November 1974, voters had reacted against Nixon and the Republicans. Many new liberals were elected to Congress, which increased the number of Jordan's political allies. She used her new circumstances to pursue antidiscrimination laws aggressively. On behalf of women, she argued for extending the deadline for states to ratify the Equal Rights Amendment. She also advocated providing Social Security benefits to home-makers.[4] And she fought restrictions on federal funding for abortions under the so-called Hyde Amendment. When she discovered that the Jordan Amendment had not made police departments integrate, she pushed a new enforcement provision through Congress.[5]

Her most influential action was the extension of the 1965 Voting Rights Act, the Voting Rights Act of 1975. The 1965 act had outlawed many practices that inhibited African Americans from voting in the Deep South. Its passage had led to a rapid increase in the number of African American and other minority politicians in state, local, and federal offices.[6]

But the act was only in force for ten years. In 1975, its extension was in trouble. For one thing, the arch-conservative James Eastland of Mississippi chaired the Senate Judiciary Committee. Eastland's committee was vital to the passage of voting-rights legislation. Gerald Ford was also a problem for the extension of the act. Ford had become president when Richard Nixon resigned. Jordan did not believe that Ford was particularly friendly to civil rights. In fact, Jordan and the rest of the Congressional Black Caucus had voted against confirming Gerald Ford as vice president because of his weak civil-rights record. Jordan feared that he would eventually become president, able to veto any civil-rights legislation should he choose.[7]

Jordan was determined to renew the law and to extend its enforcement beyond the Deep South to Texas. She had received numerous reports of voter intimidation in East Texas, which had a large African American population. Mexican Americans in Texas and the rest of the Southwest wanted bilingual ballots so that they could vote more easily. She began to lobby the Texas Congressional delegation for support of the extended civil-rights act.

It took a monumental amount of politicking to succeed, especially after state politicians in Texas discovered Jordan's intentions. Nearly all of the Texas state politicians, including the governor, were incensed that the federal government might gain oversight in its elections. But Jordan, as well as liberal and black allies, got the law through the House of Representatives. The vote was 341 to 70, well beyond the two-thirds majority needed to override a presidential veto from Gerald Ford. Because of Jordan's efforts, more than two-thirds of the Texas delegation voted for the extension of the law.[8]

Meanwhile, in the Senate, Jordan received help from Senators Mike Mansfield and Robert Byrd. They bypassed Eastland's committee and took the bill to the Senate floor. After a small compromise between the Senate and the House versions, the Voting Rights Act of 1975 was passed. President Ford reluctantly signed the bill into law.[9]

*T*hose were the most successful days of Jordan's legislative career. Watergate had created an opportunity for Jordan that she used to pursue her political beliefs. The mood of the country and of the Congress supported many of her efforts. But her satisfaction with her political career did not last long. With her greater influence came greater scrutiny of her actions. Liberal and black allies expected a lot from her.

She was not always an advocate for the poor and powerless. Jordan sometimes acted as if she had a greater duty to her constituents, some of whom were wealthy and influential. She voted to extend a $2 billion tax subsidy for the oil industry, in spite of massive oil profits in the preceding years. She also voted to deregulate natural gas. That effort failed, but its passage would have substantially raised the heating costs for more than half the country. For Jordan, these were votes that part of her constituency wanted; they were part of what got her elected by the Houston establishment.[10]

Her votes led both her liberal and her black allies to question what use she was making of her greater power in Congress. She proved even more controversial to them when she agreed to testify on behalf of John Connally at his criminal trial for bribery. Connally was no friend of Barbara Jordan. This was the same John Connally who, as governor of Texas, refused to uphold the law granting African Americans equal access to all public places.

Jordan had an even more ugly memory of Connally. In April 1968, Martin Luther King was assassinated in front of a Memphis, Tennessee, hotel room. Jordan grieved his loss. Days later, she was at a fair in San Antonio with Texas Governor Connally when he commented on the murder: "Those who live by the sword die by the sword."[11] Connally implied that King had brought on his own murder through his activism for civil rights. From that moment on, Jordan decided he was a scoundrel.

Yet she was a character witness for him in his corruption trial. Connally had a strange history in politics. He had been a powerful figure in the Texas Democratic party and a potentially strong candidate for president. But his stance on civil rights and other conservative beliefs put him at odds with many in the Democratic party establishment.

In the past six years, Connally had moved out of the Democratic party. He had become secretary of the treasury under Nixon during Nixon's first term. In Nixon's

1972 reelection campaign, he had led a Democrats for Nixon movement. Eventually, he became a Republican. Many people thought Connally would be Nixon's choice for the Republican candidate for president in 1976. Connally was riding high, filled with ambition to become the next president of the United States. Then his star fell fast. Nixon resigned, and Connally was accused of accepting a bribe to increase milk prices while he was secretary of the treasury. He was placed on trial in Washington, D.C.

Robert Strauss, the new chairman of the Democratic national party, approached Jordan about Connally. She immediately said no. But Strauss asked her to reconsider. Strauss was not only powerful but an old friend and ally of Connally in spite of Connally's behavior. Strauss believed strongly in loyalty. Jordan reconsidered. She decided that she disliked and condemned Connally for his behavior, but that was altogether different from deciding he was a crook.[12]

To her allies in Congress and elsewhere, Jordan's decision seemed unjustifiable. She began to be criticized publicly. One magazine commentator wrote, "Jordan has won another political chip, but one can't help wondering at what personal price."[13] The "political chip" was the gratitude Robert Strauss owed her.

Jordan was being attacked for compromising her values in the interest of political ambition. The criticism rankled her. Jordan may have been independent, but she also wanted the recognition and approval of liberal and black allies. The cost of her independence had usually been smaller than this. She had been called aloof and even cold because she kept herself apart from her political allies. But now the criticism had focused upon her character and her ideals.

It had happened before. She had been severely criticized for introducing Senator Robert Byrd of West Virginia during a Democratic convention in 1974. She praised him for "his sense of justice." Byrd, however, was a former member of the Ku Klux Klan who had voted against most civil-rights bills. Under fire, Jordan defended herself. People can change and we can help them to change, she said. She felt vindicated when Byrd promised her she would not regret her actions. Byrd pushed the Voting Rights Act of 1975 past Mississippi senator James Eastland and through the United States Senate.[14]

The attacks for her testimony on behalf of Connally, however, were more difficult for her to take. They came as life in Congress grew less satisfying. The Watergate hearings were more than a year past, so Jordan's celebrity status was fading. And as it did, her ability to get bills through Congress decreased. Jordan was growing weary of the struggle within the House to pass legislation she believed in. As 1976 began, President Ford repeatedly vetoed bills she favored, from public-works programs to federal funding of day care for children. Meanwhile, inflation was in double digits, and the unemployment rate was 20 percent among African American males under the age of twenty-five, rising to 40 percent among all young black males.[15] Her constituents were suffering.

Jordan had also been harboring a secret for three years. In 1973 she began to experience numbness in her feet and strange difficulties manipulating her hands and fingers. Eventually, the symptoms worsened. She was admitted to Bethesda Naval Hospital. There, medical tests strongly suggested that she had multiple sclerosis (MS). MS progressively attacks a sheath around the spinal cord that delivers nerve impulses to the muscles. It progressively disables its victims in unpredictable ways. She hid the diagnosis from the public for the rest of her life, as she did all information about her health. She was even angry with her staff when they told the *Houston Post* that she had been hospitalized. Only those closest to her, such as Nancy Earl, knew the truth. For a long time, she kept the news from her family.

But the effect of the disease was undeniable. Jordan's feet felt sluggish and were sometimes difficult to move. She wasn't her normal, energetic self. Through various medicines and a bit of luck, she avoided other symptoms until the end of 1975. Then, she experienced her second major episode of the disease. The right side of her face was briefly paralyzed.[16] Overworked and overweight, discouraged by the progression of the disease, Jordan began to rethink her life.

Nancy Earl was about to build a home in the Onion Creek area of Austin. Jordan proposed to do it with her. It would be a place Jordan could finally call her own, away from Houston and her constituents. It was also away from Washington, D.C. She would be living with her dear friend and frequent companion. Nancy Earl had been with her when she was Governor for a Day and when she was sworn in to the United States Congress. No politicians would bother her at her new home. No reporters would make it past her protective circle of friends. It would be a place to retire to at some point. Construction workers broke ground for the house in 1976.[17]

Jordan was tired of Congress and upset about criticisms when Robert Strauss asked her to give a keynote address at the 1976 Democratic National Convention.

Jimmy Carter was the likely Democratic candidate to oppose Gerald Ford. Strauss wanted John Glenn and Jordan each to give an address: "The newness of an astronaut plus the newness of a black woman, that would be an unbeatable combination," he told her.[18]

Jordan agreed to do it. The goal of a speech at the national convention gave Jordan a new sense of direction, and as the time approached, she was unexpectedly a center of attention among Democratic politicians.[19] Jimmy Carter had briefly circulated a list of potential vice presidential candidates in the media. Jordan's name was among them. Jordan did not hold out much hope it would happen. She was the most popular and powerful African American in the country, yet she thought it was still unrealistic to believe that a black woman could be nominated vice president.[20] Then came her speech at the convention in New York City, the one that brought the crowd roaring to its feet in support of her, before millions of television viewers. She still thought it was impossible as the delegates screamed "We want Barbara." But she appreciated it.

Jordan's keynote speech was a rallying cry for more than her fellow Democrats. It was a call to herself, to revive her own spirits after the frustrations of the current Congress and the difficulties of her disease. The response of the audience and of the national press rejuvenated her. She had been the star of the convention, their home-run hitter, the press had declared. Maybe, she thought, she wasn't done yet.[21]

Her reelection to Congress in 1976 was a shoo-in, so she devoted herself to helping Carter and vice-presidential candidate Walter Mondale. She campaigned enthusiastically for them even though Carter did not

Barbara Jordan and Jimmy Carter in 1976. Jordan introduced Carter at the Democratic National Convention and recommended his nomination for president.

impress her; Ford and the Republicans impressed her less.[22] She loved being out among the people. She also felt as if she were out there campaigning for herself for president, going through the motions a candidate might make, building the support and the applause.

In the end, however, it was Carter who appeared on the ballot. He beat Gerald Ford by a narrow margin in

November 1976. In six key states, Jordan contributed mightily to black voter turnout. In four of them, including Texas, the black vote made the difference between victory and defeat for Carter.[23] After the election, Carter met with Jordan about a position in his administration. She was prepared for him. She told Carter that she would accept only the position of attorney general of the United States. As attorney general, she would oversee enforcement of civil-rights laws as well as other federal statutes. There she believed she could further her goals.[24]

Jimmy Carter wasn't enthusiastic. He asked her if she was interested in becoming the representative to the United Nations. She told him she had no interest in the United Nations; she had no experience in foreign relations. Soon, it became clear to Carter that Jordan meant what she said: She would accept only the position of attorney general. The meeting was brief.

Jordan returned to Congress for her third term in January 1977. The United States Senate, the House of Representatives, and the presidency were all controlled by Democrats. But they quickly began to fight among themselves. It discouraged Jordan. Her weight was now dropping from multiple sclerosis. It became more difficult for her to walk. She began to ask herself, "How many times do you repeat this performance? How many times do you keep presenting a bill and getting it passed and getting the president to sign it?"[25] She was still devoted to improving civil-rights legislation. But she became less focused on the issues of her congressional district and more interested in issues she considered "national in scope."[26] Soaring medical costs and the economy were two of her concerns.

Marian Anderson and Barbara Jordan received honorary degrees from Harvard University, June 1977.

Her greatest interest, however, was citizen participation in politics. It was what she spoke about when Harvard invited her to give its commencement address in June 1977. At Harvard, she declared that ordinary citizens were not as able to participate in the politics of the country as they once had been. Politicians in Washington weren't governing for the people; instead they were more committed to themselves. Government had become a "spectator sport" for most people. She asked for the "reinclusion of people in their government."[27]

In the months following her speech, Jordan began to think that she didn't need to be an elected public official to address the issues that most interested her. If anything, public office made it more difficult for her to energize greater public participation.[28] Her life had shifted ground for many reasons: her discouragement with Washington, her belief in the importance of public participation, her dislike of criticism, her disease, her need for greater privacy. In December 1977, Barbara Jordan announced she would not run for a fourth term in Congress.

Afterword

In January 1979, Barbara Jordan left public life to become professor of public policy at the Lyndon Baines Johnson School of Public Affairs at the University of Texas, Austin. She was forty-three years old and still a phenomenon in the eyes of the nation. A *People* magazine survey reported that Americans chose her as their top pick to become the first woman president of the United States.[1]

In Austin, she settled into her home with Nancy Earl and began her new life as a private citizen and college teacher. She wrote a combination biography and memoir with the novelist Shelby Hearon. Meanwhile, she fiercely guarded her privacy. Within the first few days of her arrival in Austin, a Dallas newspaper article reported that she had a fatal disease. An angry Jordan held a news conference where she made it clear that the article was false and that any questions about her health were wholly inappropriate.[2]

Her health had continued to decline. By 1979, she walked with the aid of a cane, which, she explained to anyone who asked, was because of a bad knee.[3] A year later, she needed a wheelchair. It was difficult for her to get in and out of cars. She relied upon students to help her get back and forth to the university. Yet she was devoted to her students, and she continued to teach until her death.[4]

Out of the limelight of public office, Jordan surrounded herself with her closest friends. She attended dinner parties thrown by the dean of the LBJ School of Public Affairs. She talked politics and law with her fellow faculty members. She was an enormously popular teacher. She became an avid fan and honorary coach of the University of Texas women's basketball team, the Lady Longhorns. When she wasn't socializing, she read in her spacious home or swam in her pool.[5]

In her first years in Austin, Jordan avoided any involvement in electoral politics. She even refused to endorse President Jimmy Carter's reelection attempt in 1980. Meanwhile, she cofounded the liberal advocacy group People for the American Way. Then, in 1984, she began to make public appearances on behalf of selected candidates for Congress and the Senate: Senator Bill Bradley of New Jersey; and Lloyd Doggett, who opposed incumbent Senator Phil Gramm of Texas.[6]

In 1987 she made her most visible reappearance in public life. She was one of the chief opponents to Robert Bork, President Ronald Reagan's choice for a vacant position on the U.S. Supreme Court. As a law professor, Bork had declared that a number of Supreme Court decisions misread the Constitution. Bork believed that many judges had tried to extended the

Professor of Public Policy Barbara Jordan,
University of Texas at Austin

meaning of the Constitution to fit modern times. To Bork, that violated the "original meaning" that the writers of the Constitution intended. He did not believe there was a constitutional right to privacy, and he said that he would have voted against Supreme Court decisions that required the reform of legislative districts in the South—the very decisions that led to Barbara Jordan's election to the Texas Senate.

Along with a select number of black leaders and liberals, Barbara Jordan testified before the Senate Judiciary Committee. The committee's job was to screen judicial candidates and pass them on to the full Senate, where they were confirmed or rejected. Before the committee, Jordan declared her wholesale opposition to Bork's nomination. Bork, she said, wanted to return the country to a time where the federal courts saw no duty to protect the rights of minorities in the United States. She said that she could not stand by and let that happen.[7] On prime-time television news programs, Jordan debated leading Republican supporters of Bork's candidacy. Eventually, Bork's nomination was rejected by the Senate.

The victory reawakened Jordan's interest in an active political life. Through much of the summer of 1988, she made public appearances as a political and social commentator on radio and television stations. She began campaigning for the Democratic candidates for president and vice president, Michael Dukakis and Lloyd Bentsen, and she gave the nominating speech for Bentsen at the Democratic National Convention.[8]

Later that summer, Jordan's health failed her in a frightening way. As she sat by the edge of the swimming pool of her home, she suffered cardiac arrest and blacked out, falling into the pool. Nancy Earl discovered Jordan motionless in the water. She wasn't breathing, and she had no pulse. Rushed to the hospital, Jordan miraculously survived the incident. Rumors circulated in the media that the wheelchair-bound Jordan attempted to commit suicide. Yet Jordan was not depressed about her health or her life. Within a month, she was co-chairing the Dukakis-Bentsen campaign in Texas.[9]

In spite of her increasing physical difficulties, Jordan continued to participate in politics. When Bill Clinton was nominated for president in 1992, Jordan gave a keynote address at the Democratic National Convention. She attended Clinton's inauguration in 1992, and a year later, she accepted Clinton's request that she be chairperson of the United States Commission on Immigration Reform.

But her health worsened. In 1994 she contracted leukemia, a fatal illness. She led the commission for another year while it issued two reports. The leukemia ended her public activities, and by the winter of 1995, she was weak and growing weaker. There was little chance she would recover.[10] On January 17, 1996, Barbara Jordan died. She was a month away from her sixtieth birthday.

Three days later, family members, friends, and other mourners packed Good Hope Missionary Baptist Church. President Bill Clinton, former Texas governor Ann Richards, actress Cicely Tyson, and Jordan's debate coach Tom Freeman all eulogized her. In Washington, a memorial service drew tributes from Republicans and Democrats alike. In the state cemetery in Austin, Texas—now integrated thanks to her efforts in the Texas Senate—Barbara Jordan's body was laid to rest.[11]

Jordan received the Presidential Medal of Freedom in 1994 from President Bill Clinton.

Barbara Jordan's private life remains the guarded memory of her family and friends. But her life as a politician has an enduring place in the memory of the country. In the last years of her life, she received numerous awards that guarantee she will forever be associated with the ideals she declared during her keynote address at the Democratic National Convention in 1976. The Houston federal building and post office was named for her, as were streets and schools throughout the country. Then, in 1994, President Bill Clinton gave her the highest award the federal government bestows upon a civilian, the Presidential Medal of Freedom.[12] Together, these honors ensure that in death as in life, she will be remembered as a pioneer among black women and a symbol of the hope for equality among all Americans.

Source Notes

CHAPTER 1

1. Barbara Jordan and Shelby Hearon, *Barbara Jordan: A Self-Portrait* (Garden City, NY: Doubleday & Company, 1979), pp. 192–199.

2. Jordan and Hearon, p. 227.

3. Mary Beth Rogers, *Barbara Jordan: An American Hero* (New York: Bantam Books, 1998), p. 269.

4. Rogers, p. 231

5. Rogers, pp. 232–233.

6. Rogers, pp. 244.

CHAPTER 2

1. B.C. Robison, *Birds of Houston* (Houston: University of Rice Press, 1990), pp. 11, 66; and David G. McComb *Houston: A History* (Austin: University of Texas Press, 1969), pp. 4, 12.

2. James E. Buchanan, ed., *Houston: A Chronological and Documentary History, 1519–1970.* Dobbs Ferry, NY: Oceana Publications, Inc., 1975), p. 4.

3. Alwyn Barr, *Black Texans: A History of African Americans in Texas, 1528–1995* (Norman: University of Oklahoma Press, 1996), p. 1. Although Barr uses the name Estevan, many sources use the name Estevanico. See, for example, Donald E. Chipman, "Dorantes de Carranza, Andres," Handbook of Texas Online, University of Texas at Austin and Texas State Historical Association. Feb. 15, 1999
   <http://www.tsha.utexas.edu/handbook/>.

4. Barr, p. 3.

5. Barr, p. 14.

6. Barr, p. 15.

7. Barr, p. 9.

8. Barr, p. 43.

9. Lawrence D. Rice, *The Negro in Texas, 1874–1900* (Baton Rouge: Louisiana State University Press, 1971), pp. 184–185.

10. Barr, p. 113.

11. Howard Beeth and Cary D. Wintz, eds., *Black Dixie: Afro-Texan History and Culture in Houston* (College Station: Texas A&M University Press, 1992), pp. 4, 88.

12. Ruth Winegarten. *Black Texas Women: 150 Years of Trial and Triumph* (Austin: University of Texas Press, 1995).

13. Winegarten, pp. 88, 91.

14. Winegarten, pp. 90, 93–94.

15. Winegarten, p. 98.

16. Buchanan, pp. 106–107.

CHAPTER 3

1. Barbara Jordan and Shelby Hearon, *Barbara Jordan: A Self-Portrait* (Garden City, NY: Doubleday & Company, 1979), pp. 30–31.

2. David Levering Lewis, *W.E.B. Du Bois: Biography of a*

Race, 1868–1919 (New York: Henry Holt and Company, 1993), p. 175.

3. Jordan and Hearon, p. 30.

4. Jordan and Hearon, p. 26.

5. Jordan and Hearon, p. 29.

6. Taylor Branch, *Parting the Waters: America in the King Years, 1954–1963* (New York: Simon & Schuster, 1988), p. 3.

7. Mary Beth Rogers, *Barbara Jordan: An American Hero* (New York: Bantam Books, 1998), p. 23.

8. Rogers, pp. 27, 33.

9. Jordan and Hearon, p. 46.

10. Jordan and Hearon, p.4.

11. Jordan and Hearon, pp. 4–6.

12. Jordan and Hearon, p. 6.

13. Jordan and Hearon, pp. 9–11.

14. Jordan and Hearon, p. 8.

15. Jordan and Hearon, p. 12.

16. Rogers, pp. 8–10.

17. Jordan and Hearon, p. 11.

18. Jordan and Hearon, p. 15.

19. Jordan and Hearon, pp. 16.

20. Jordan and Hearon, p. 15.

21. Jordan and Hearon, pp. 17–19.

22. Jordan and Hearon, pp. 20–21.

23. Jordan and Hearon, p. 21.

24. Jordan and Hearon, p. 8.

25. Jordan and Hearon, pp. 10, 22.

26. Jordan and Hearon, p. 7.

27. Jordan and Hearon, p. 73.

CHAPTER 4

1. Barbara Jordan and Shelby Hearon, *Barbara Jordan: A Self-Portrait* (Garden City, NY: Doubleday & Company, 1979), pp. 31–32.

2. Jordan and Hearon, p. 33.

3. Jordan and Hearon, p. 34.

4. Jordan and Hearon, p. 35.

5. Jordan and Hearon, pp. 33–34.

6. Mary Beth Rogers, *Barbara Jordan: An American Hero* (New York: Bantam Books, 1998), p. 32.

7. William Broyles, "The Making of Barbara Jordan," *Texas Monthly,* October 1976. Quoted in Rogers, p. 32.

8. Jordan and Hearon, p. 44.

9. Jordan and Hearon, p. 28.

10. Jordan and Hearon, p. 47.

11. Jordan and Hearon, p. 36.

12. Jordan and Hearon, pp. 35–37.

13. Rogers, p. 27.

14. Rogers, pp. 35–37.

15. Rogers, p. 38.

16. Rogers, p. 34.

17. Jordan and Hearon, pp. 39–40.

18. Jordan and Hearon, p. 41.

19. Jordan and Hearon, p. 43.

20. Rogers, p. 37.

21. Rogers, p. 42.

22. Jordan and Hearon, p. 43.

23. Rogers, p. 33.

24. Quoted in Rogers, p. 33.

CHAPTER 5

1. Mary Beth Rogers, *Barbara Jordan: An American Hero* (New York: Bantam Books, 1998), p. 29.

2. William H. Robinson. *Phillis Wheatley and Her Writings* (New York: Garland Publishing, 1984).

3. Barbara Jordan and Shelby Hearon, *Barbara Jordan: A Self-Portrait* (Garden City, NY: Doubleday & Company, 1979), p. 57.

4. Jordan and Hearon, pp. 55–56.

5. Jordan and Hearon, pp. 58–59.

6. Jordan and Hearon, p. 56.

7. Jordan and Hearon, p. 57; and Rogers, p. 39

8. Rogers, p. 29.

9. Jordan and Hearon, p. 62

10. Jordan and Hearon, p. 65.

11. Jordan and Hearon, p. 22.

12. Jordan and Hearon, p. 62.

13. Jordan and Hearon, p. 22.

14. Jordan and Hearon, p. 63.

15. Jordan and Hearon, p. 54.

16. Jordan and Hearon, pp. 63–64.

17. Rogers, pp. 47–48.

18. Taylor Branch, *Parting the Waters: America in the King Years, 1954–1963* (New York: Simon & Schuster, 1988), p. 13.

19. Rogers, p. 30.

20. After a successful career arguing before the Supreme court on behalf of the NAACP, Marshall was appointed to it by President Lyndon B. Johnson and went on to become one of the most famous Supreme Court justices of the late twentieth century. For more on Marshall, see Juan Williams, *Thurgood Marshall: American Revolutionary* (New York: Random House, 1998).

21. Williams, pp. 110–112; and Howard Beeth and Cary D. Wintz, eds., *Black Dixie: Afro-Texan History and Culture in Houston* (College Station: Texas A&M University Press, 1992), p. 158.

22. Williams, pp. 175–176, 180–185.

23. Rogers, p. 30.

24. Jordan and Hearon, p. 61.

25. Jordan and Hearon, pp. 64–65.

26. Jordan and Hearon, pp. 66–67.

27. Rogers, p. 41.

28. Jordan and Hearon, pp. 68–69.

29. Jordan and Hearon, pp. 71–72.

30. Rogers, p. 43.

CHAPTER 6

1. Barbara Jordan and Shelby Hearon, *Barbara Jordan: A Self-Portrait* (Garden City, NY: Doubleday & Company, 1979), p. 75.

2. Jordan and Hearon, p. 76.

3. Ibid.

4. Jordan and Hearon, p. 77 and Mary Beth Rogers, *Barbara Jordan: An American Hero* (New York: Bantam Books, 1998), p. 51.

5. Jordan and Hearon, pp. 77–78.

6. Jordan and Hearon, p. 77.

7. Jordan and Hearon, p. 82.

8. Jordan and Hearon, pp. 77–79.

9. Albert P. Blaustein and Robert L. Zangiando, eds., *Civil Rights and African Americans* (Evanston, IL: Northwestern University Press, 1998), pp. 433–437. For more documents on the case, see pp. 418–432 and 438–442. Quoted in Jordan and Hearon, pp. 79–80.

10. Jordan and Hearon, p. 80.

11. David Montejano, *Anglos and Mexicans in the Making of Texas, 1836–1986.* (Austin: University of Texas Press, 1987), p. 275; Quoted in Rogers, 58.

12. Taylor Branch, *Parting the Waters: America in the King Years, 1954–1963* (New York: Simon & Schuster, 1988), pp. 128–205.

13. Jordan and Hearon, p. 81.

14. Jordan and Hearon. p. 76.

15. Jordan and Hearon, p. 81.

16. Jordan and Hearon, p. 75.

17. Rogers, p. 50.

18. Jordan and Hearon, p. 82.

19. Jordan and Hearon, p. 83.

20. Rogers, p. 63.

21. Ibid.

22. Jordan and Hearon, pp. 85–86, 90.

23. Ibid., pp. 89–91.

24. Rogers, p. 63; and Jordan and Hearon, p. 92.

25. Jordan and Hearon, p. 93–94.

26. Jordan and Hearon, p. 95.

27. Branch, pp. 222–225.

28. Jordan and Hearon, pp. 96–97; and Rogers, p. 69.

29. Jordan and Hearon, p. 23; and Rogers, pp. 72–73.

30. Rogers, p. 72.

31. Jordan and Hearon, p. 98.

32. Jordan and Hearon, pp. 107–108.

CHAPTER 7

1. Joe R. Feagin, *Free Enterprise City: Houston in Political-Economic Perspective.* New Brunswick, NJ: Rutgers University Press, 1988, 93; Quoted in Mary Beth Rogers, *Barbara Jordan: An American Hero* (New York: Bantam Books, 1998), pp. 74–75.

2. Rogers, p. 75, and Alwyn Barr, *Black Texans: A History of African Americans in Texas, 1528–1995* (Norman: University of Oklahoma Press, 1996), p. 199.

3. Barr, pp. 202, 190.

4. Barr, pp. 100–101.

5. Taylor Branch, *Parting the Waters: America in the King Years, 1954–1963* (New York: Simon & Schuster, 1988), pp. 271–273.

6. Kenneth F. Jensen. "The Houston Sit-In Movement of 1960-1961," in Howard Beeth and Cary D. Wintz, eds., *Black Dixie: Afro-Texan History and Culture in Houston* (College Station: Texas A&M University Press, 1992), pp. 211–222.

7. Charlotte Phelan, "State Senator Barbara Jordan Wins Her Battles Through the System." *Houston Post*, May 24, 1970. Quoted in Rogers, p. 101.

8. Quoted in Rogers. See also James S. Hirsch, "Driving Miss Jordan," *The Wall Street Journal*, January 20, 1996.

9. Rogers, p. 81.

10. Barbara Jordan and Shelby Hearon, *Barbara Jordan: A Self-Portrait* (Garden City, NY: Doubleday & Company, 1979), p. 122.

11. Jordan and Hearon, pp. 110–111.

12. Rogers, pp. 80–81; and Jordan and Hearon, p. 110.

13. Rogers, pp. 86, 83.

14. Jordan and Hearon, p. 112.

15. Rogers, pp. 84, 87.

16. Jordan and Hearon, pp. 112–114.

17. Jordan and Hearon, 151. Quoted in Rogers, p. 89.

18. Rogers, p. 89; and Jordan and Hearon, pp. 115–16.

19. Jordan and Hearon, p. 116.

20. Branch, pp. 560–600, 846–887.

21. Jordan and Hearon, pp. 116–117.

22. Jordan and Hearon., p. 122.

23. Jordan and Hearon, pp. 117–118.

24. Jordan and Hearon, p. 118.

25. Jordan and Hearon, p. 119.

26. Rogers, pp. 97–98.

27. Rogers, pp. 98–100.

28. Quoted in Jordan and Hearon, p. 124.

29. Albert P. Blaustein and Robert L. Zangiando, eds., *Civil Rights and African Americans* (Evanston, IL: Northwestern University Press, 1998), pp. 524–550.

30. Rogers, p. 96.

31. Jordan and Hearon, pp. 120–122.

32. Rogers, pp. 102–103.

33. Jordan and Hearon, pp. 130–132.

34. Jordan and Hearon, p. 133.

35. Jordan and Hearon, p. 134.

36. Rogers, p. 106; One other African American—Joe Lockridge—was elected from the Dallas area.

37. Rogers, pp. 106-107.

CHAPTER 8

1. Mary Beth Rogers, *Barbara Jordan: An American Hero* (New York: Bantam Books, 1998), p. 109.

2. Rogers, p. 111.

3. Rogers, p. 112.

4. In most parts of the country, the Democrats believed more strongly than Republicans in the power of the federal government. At the federal level, the Democrats controlled the U.S. House of Representatives, the Senate, and the presidency during most of the 1960s. They had also led the passage of the Civil Rights Act of 1964 and the Voting Rights Act of 1965. In 1999,

Republicans became the dominant party in many southern states.

5. Rogers, p. 113.

6. Barbara Jordan and Shelby Hearon, *Barbara Jordan: A Self-Portrait* (Garden City, NY: Doubleday & Company, 1979), p. 138.

7. Jordan and Hearon, p. 140.

8. Rogers, pp. 113–114.

9. Jordan and Hearon, p. 141.

10. Jordan and Hearon; and Rogers, p. 115.

11. Rogers, p. 123.

12. Jordan and Hearon, p. 140.

13. Jordan and Hearon, p. 148.

14. Rogers, p. 117.

15. Ibid.

16. Jordan and Hearon, p. 140.

17. Jordan and Hearon, p. 144.

18. Jordan and Hearon, p. 148.

19. Rogers, p. 115.

20. Jordan and Hearon, pp. 142–144.

21. Jordan and Hearon, pp. 149–150.

22. Jordan and Hearon, p. 152.

CHAPTER 9

1. Mary Beth Rogers, *Barbara Jordan: An American Hero* (New York: Bantam Books, 1998), p. 119.

2. Rogers, p.125.

3. Rogers, p. 132.

4. Barbara Jordan and Shelby Hearon, *Barbara Jordan: A Self-Portrait* (Garden City, NY: Doubleday & Company, 1979), p. 146.

5. Jordan and Hearon, p. 148.

6. Robert A. Caro, *The Years of Lyndon Johnson: Means of Ascent* (New York: Oxford, 1999), p. xvii.

7. Caro, pp. xix–xx.

8. Caro, pp. xx–xxi.

9. Caro, pp. xxiii–xxiv.

10. Caro, p. xxv.

11. Jordan and Hearon, p.147.

12. Rogers, p. 148.

13. Ira B. Bryant, *Barbara Charline Jordan: From the Ghetto to the Capitol.* (Houston: D. Armstrong Company, 1975), pp. 18–20; and Rogers, p. 189.

14. Jordan and Hearon, p. 149.

15. Rogers, p. 148.

16. Jordan and Hearon, p. 158.

17. Jordan and Hearon, p. 153.

18. Rogers, pp. 136–138.

19. Rogers, pp. 140–141.

20. Jordan and Hearon, pp. 154–155.

21. Rogers, pp. 156–158.

22. Jordan and Hearon, pp. 157–158.

23. Jordan and Hearon, p.159.

24. Rogers, p. 163.

25. Jordan, pp. 155–156.

26. Rogers, pp. 161–162.

27. Jordan and Hearon, p. 156.

28. Rogers, pp. 160, 162, 165.

29. Jordan and Hearon, p. 161.

30. Jordan and Hearon, p. 166.

31. Rogers, pp. 144, 168.

32. Jordan and Hearon, pp. 167–169.

CHAPTER 10

1. Barbara Jordan and Shelby Hearon, *Barbara Jordan: A Self-Portrait* (Garden City, NY: Doubleday & Company, 1979), pp. 177–178.

2. Mary Beth Rogers, *Barbara Jordan: An American Hero* (New York: Bantam Books, 1998), p. 178.

3. Jordan and Hearon, p. 179.

4. Rogers, pp. 176–177.

5. Rogers, pp. 185–187.

6. Rogers, p. 186.

7. Jordan and Hearon, pp. 180–181.

8. Rogers, p. 174.

9. Jordan and Hearon, p. 181.

10. Jordan and Hearon, p. 203, and Rogers, p.187.

11. Rogers, p. 187.

12. Rogers, p. 251.

13. Rogers, p. 187.

14. Paula Giddings, "Will the Real Barbara Jordan Please Stand," *Encore American and Worldwide News*, May 9, 1977. Quoted in Rogers, p. 188.

15. Jordan and Hearon, pp. 205–206. See also Rogers, pp. 193–194.

16. Carl Bernstein and Bob Woodward. *All the President's Men*, (New York: Simon & Schuster, 1994), pp. 15–19.

17. Rogers, p. 196.

18. Jordan and Hearon, p. 188.

19. Jordan and Hearon, pp. 184–185.

20. Rogers, p. 207.

21. Jordan and Hearon, p. 183; and Rogers, p. 208.

22. Jordan and Hearon, p.184; and Rogers, p. 211.

23. Jordan and Hearon, p.192.

24. Rogers, pp. 213–214.

25. Jordan and Hearon, p. 187.

26. Jordan and Hearon, pp. 186–91.

27. Jordan and Hearon, pp. 194–99; and Rogers, p. 217.

28. Rogers, pp. 219–22. See also *Summer of Judgment-Impeachment Hearings.* Film Documentary. Prod. Greater Washington Educational Telecommunications Associates (WETA-Washington), Charles McDowell, narrator, 1984. Cited in Rogers, p. 222.

CHAPTER 11

1. Barbara Jordan and Shelby Hearon, *Barbara Jordan: A Self-Portrait* (Garden City, NY: Doubleday & Company, 1979), p. 204.

2. Mary Beth Rogers, *Barbara Jordan: An American Hero* (New York: Bantam Books, 1998), p. 248.

3. Rogers, p. 250.

4. Jordan and Hearon, pp. 216–217; and Rogers, p. 189.

5. Jordan and Hearon, p. 207.

6. Jordan and Hearon, pp. 209–212.

7. Rogers, p. 198.

8. Rogers, p. 246

9. Jordan and Hearon, p. 211.

10. Rogers, pp. 228–230.

11. Jordan and Hearon, p. 152.

12. Jordan and Hearon, pp. 221–224.

13. Jordan and Hearon, p. 226.

14. Rogers, pp. 246–247.

15. Rogers, pp. 257–258.

16. Ibid., pp. 198–202.

17. Jordan and Hearon, pp. 237–239; and Rogers, pp. 253–54.

18. Jordan and Hearon, pp. 228–229.

19. Jordan and Hearon, p. 227.

20. Rogers, pp. 261–262.

21. Rogers, pp. 270–271.

22. Jordan and Hearon, p. 243.

23. Rogers, p. 276.

24. Jordan and Hearon, pp. 244–245.

25. Jordan and Hearon, p. 247.

26. Jordan and Hearon, p. 265.

27. Jordan and Hearon, p. 266.

28. Jordan and Hearon, p. 249.

AFTERWORD

1. "Jordan Top Pick to Head Nation," *Austin Citizen*, March 20, 1998; quoted in Rogers, p. 305.

2. Mary Beth Rogers, *Barbara Jordan: An American Hero* (New York: Bantam Books, 1998), pp. 301–03.

3. Rogers, p. 204

4. Rogers, pp. 314–315.

5. Rogers, pp. 318–319.

6. Rogers, pp. 312, 321.

7. Rogers, p. 329.

8. Rogers, pp. 330–332.

9. Rogers, pp. 332–335.

10. Rogers, p. 351.

11. Rogers, p. 355.

12. Rogers, pp. 322, 344, 349

Bibliography and Web Sites

Barr, Alwyn. *Black Texans: A History of African Americans in Texas, 1528–1995.* Norman: University of Oklahoma Press, 1973.

Beeth, Howard, and Cary D. Wintz, editors. *Black Dixie: Afro-Texan History and Culture in Houston.* College Station: Texas A&M University Press, 1992.

Bernstein, Carl, and Bob Woodward. *All the President's Men.* New York: Simon & Schuster, 1977.

Blaustein, Albert P., and Robert L. Zangiando, editors. *Civil Rights and African Americans.* Evanston, IL: Northwestern University Press, 1998.

Branch, Taylor. *Parting the Waters: America in the King Years, 1954–1963.* New York: Simon & Schuster, 1988.

Broyles, William. "The Making of Barbara Jordan," *Texas Monthly,* October 1976.

Bryant, Ira B. *Barbara Charline Jordan: From the Ghetto to the Capitol.* Houston: D. Armstrong Company, 1975.

Buchanan, James E., editor. *Houston: A Chronological and Documentary History, 1519–1970*. Dobbs Ferry, NY: Oceana Publications, Inc., 1975.

Caro, Robert A. *The Years of Lyndon Johnson: Means of Ascent*. New York: Oxford, 1999.

Chipman, Donald E. "Dorantes de Carranza, Andres. *Handbook of Texas Online*. University of Texas at Austin and Texas State Historical Association. Feb. 15, 1999 <http://www.tsha.utexas.edu/handbook/>.

Feagin, Joe R. *Free Enterprise City: Houston in Political-Economic Perspective*. New Brunswick, NJ: Rutgers University Press, 1988.

Giddings, Paula. "Will the Real Barbara Jordan Please Stand?" *Encore American and Worldwide News*, May 9, 1977.

Hirsch, James S. "Driving Miss Jordan," *The Wall Street Journal*, January 20, 1996.

Jordan, Barbara, and Shelby Hearon. *Barbara Jordan: A Self-Portrait*. Garden City, New York: Doubleday & Company, 1979.

Lewis, David Levering. *W. E. B. Du Bois: Biography of a Race, 1868–1919*. New York: Henry Holt and Company, 1993.

McComb, David G. *Houston: A History*. Austin: University of Texas Press, 1969.

Montejano, David. *Anglos and Mexicans in the Making of Texas, 1836–1986*. Austin: University of Texas Press, 1987.

Phelan, Charlotte. "State Senator Barbara Jordan Wins Her Battles Through the System," *Houston Post*, May 24, 1970.

Proceedings and Debates of the Ninety-Third Congress, First Session, Congressional Record. Vol. 119, April 18, 1973.

Rice, Lawrence D. *The Negro in Texas, 1874–1900*. Baton Rouge: Louisiana State University Press, 1971.

Robinson, William H. *Phillis Wheatley and Her Writings*. New York: Garland Publishing, 1984.

Robison, B.C. *Birds of Houston*. Houston: Rice University Press, 1990.

Rogers, Mary Beth. *Barbara Jordan: An American Hero*. New York: Bantam Books, 1998.

Summer of Judgment—Impeachment Hearings. Film Documentary. Greater Washington Educational Telecommunications Associates (WETA-Washington). Charles McDowell, narrator, 1984.

Williams, Juan. *Thurgood Marshall: American Revolutionary*. New York: Random House, 1998.

Winegarten, Ruth. *Black Texas Women: 150 Years of Trial and Triumph*. (Austin: University of Texas Press, 1995).

INTERNET INFORMATION

Internet information changes often. To find information on Barbara Jordan try a keyword search. The following Web sites had links to many other pages.

http://www.elf.net/bjordan/

http://www.riceinfo.rice.edu/armadillo/Texas/jordan.html

Index